Are you missing
what matters most?

Visionary Marriage

capture a God-sized vision for your marriage

by Rob & Amy Rienow

randall house

114 Bush Rd | Nashville, TN 37217
randallhouse.com

Visionary Marriage

© 2010 Rob and Amy Rienow

Published by Randall House
114 Bush Road
Nashville, TN 37217

ISBN 9780892656042

Printed in the United States of America

Dedication

To RW, Lissy, JD, Laynie, Milly, and Ray.

We pray that you will receive the faith passed down to you, and pass it to your children, grandchildren, and beyond.

Acknowledgments

All thanks to God, who by His grace, has kept our marriage and family together, and given us the Bible as an all-sufficient guide for our lives.

We are grateful for our parents, John and Jean, and Angie and Jack who love each other and have encouraged us in our marriage. Your prayers for us have been powerful.

Thanks to our kids, RW, Lissy, JD, Laynie, and Milly for their encouragement, patience, and extra hard work, particularly in caring for baby Ray.

Many family members were invaluable to us in providing editing and critique. Mom and Jack, thank you for your great editorial work each step of the way. Mom (Diehl), thank you for your thoughtful input. Your insights helped improve the message. Cathy, we knew it would come in handy having an English teacher in the family! We know how busy you are and your help means a lot to us. Marc and Jill, John and Meg, Emily and Luke—thanks for your prayers.

Thanks to our small group—the Nelsons, Thompsons, Chamberlains, Bickharts, Ohs, and McAuleys. We appreciate your friendship, prayers, meals, and help with the kids over these past few months. Your help has been invaluable to us. So many friends have been lifting us up in prayer—Chris and Laura, Stephanie, Jeff and Laurie, Andrew and Dana, Drew and Gina, Vance and Andrea, Michael and Sarah, Dave and Jean, and Randy and Christy. The list could go on. We hope we didn't forget anyone. Our whole church family at Wheaton Bible Church has been lifting us up in prayer during these challenging months after the birth of baby Ray.

We also want to express our appreciation to Amber and Jaclyn Agnew, and Katie and Beth Gottlieb. You have given us so much time and love, blessing our home and our children.

Last but not least, thanks to the entire team at Randall House Publishers, who believe in God's design for church and family to partner together to reach the world. We are glad to be a part of your team to move this mission and vision forward, for the glory of God!

Table of Contents

Preface

Our eyes met across a crowded room. Really! It was August 28, 1993. We were both standing in our graduate school student commons. Our eyes met. We shared a moment of attraction. I (Rob) was too much of a chicken to ask Amy out on a date. Two long months later, it took a mutual friend to encourage me to finally do it. We met for lunch after church then went back to her house to meet her parents.

Five months later we were engaged, and in another five months we were married. It is hard to believe, but we have now celebrated our fifteenth wedding anniversary, and God has blessed us with six children—three boys and three girls. There is a lot of joy in our life, but there has also been struggle and heartache.

Amy's Story

I am thankful to have grown up in a home with two parents who are in love and committed to each other. My mother was a Christian during my childhood years, but it was not until after Rob and I married that my father also trusted Christ. My parents loved me, and loved each other, but I didn't have the blessing of seeing a Christian marriage in action while I grew up in their home.

Even though I trusted Christ when I was very young, my views on marriage and family were shaped by the American culture of the 1970s and 1980s. When I was a little girl, I dreamed of many things. I wanted to be a dancer, a singer, and a writer. Yet above all these things, I wanted to be a wife and a mother. I can remember playing house, playing with baby dolls and pretending to cook. One of my favorite picture books was *The Maggie B.* It was about a little girl who had a wish come true. Her wish was to be on a boat with her baby brother. She would cook his food, bathe him, and take care of his needs. The "Maggie B" was her own little house on the sea. This was one of my favorite books, and I can remember pretending my bed was a boat as I acted out the story.

Then the question began to come, "Amy, what do you want to be when you grow up?" I caught on pretty quickly that the *right* answer was not that I wanted to be a wife and mother. The answer needed to be some sort of occupation. A wife and a mother is not what you are going to *be* when you grow up. You may get married and you may have children, but that is not what you are going to *be.* I was eventually encouraged by teachers, friends and family members that I would be an excellent counselor. So I set a course to study psychology. It's funny; when I was little I never did dream about being a counselor.

When Rob and I began our relationship, I joined him in his youth ministry at the church. Now I was a wife, a therapist, a youth worker, and then God blessed us with children. It was not until we had three kids that I realized I was poorly prepared for the ministry of being a wife and mother. This was really what I had always wanted to *be,* not a therapist or a youth worker. The message I was taught repeatedly in school was to focus on preparing for a career. Being a wife and a mother would just fit in accordingly. This was not true. First of all, I had very little training on what it meant to manage a household, much less cook! I had never been taught to serve my husband. Unfortunately, all of my academic training had not prepared me to excel at what I had always dreamed of being, a wife and mother.

From the beginning of our marriage, our home life felt chaotic to me. As a couple, we were always on the go. Home did not occupy any real space in our hearts or our schedule. Home was simply the staging ground for the next activity. Through a major crash–physically, emotionally, and spiritually–God brought me to the place of realizing that things needed to change. My heart needed changing. We needed peace in our home. The only way to have peace in our home was for someone to *be* at home. That someone was me.

Although I had been reading the Bible ever since I was a little girl, I began to read His Word as my manual for becoming the wife and mother that He wanted me to be. I am thankful that God interrupted the plans and priorities I had for my life in order to teach me His plans and priorities for my life. It was not easy having my views challenged and tested by God's Word. In fact, I had no conception that a biblical view about the role of a Christian wife was any different from the way I was living. I look forward to sharing more of my story with you in the pages ahead, and more importantly to explore the life-changing calling God gives to us as wives and mothers.

Through a major crash—physically, emotionally, and spiritually–God brought me to the place of realizing that things needed to change.

Rob's Story

I grew up in Connecticut. My father was my mother's second husband. My mother was my father's fourth wife. Neither of them were believers when they got married. By God's grace, my mother came to Christ when I was just three-months-old. From that point forward, she did her best to impress my heart with a love for Jesus. Tragically, my parents divorced when I was in high school. The divorce was very painful for my brother and me. Even worse than the divorce was the discovery that my father had been unfaithful. As a young man, I was devastated. It took God many years of working in my heart to bring me to a place of forgiveness. My dad died in 2008 at the age of 90. Miraculously, three weeks before he died, he repented of his sins and put his faith in Christ. His salvation is the greatest miracle I have ever seen and I can't wait to see him in Heaven.

I never had the blessing of seeing a visionary Christian marriage in action. In fact, my brother Marc and I are the first Christian men in our family. Without a legacy to build upon, I had a shallow vision for what it meant to be a husband and father. To say that I had a lot of growing to do would be a major understatement. But this is one of the great things about God. It doesn't matter where you have been, what you have done, or what kind of home you come from. Our family backgrounds do not doom us to failure. His grace and forgiveness can overcome any sin or any destructive generational pattern. His Word can bring vision and divine purpose into any heart.

Without a legacy to build upon, I had a shallow vision for what it meant to be a husband and father.

During the time of my parents' divorce, I sensed God calling me into youth ministry. I began serving on the pastoral staff at Wheaton Bible Church in 1992, and continue to serve there now in the role of Family Pastor. It sounds terrible to admit, but my ministry at church was my first love. It was not that I didn't love Amy and the kids, but my passion, energy, leadership, and focus was at work. Amy and the kids got the scraps. I was a leader at church, and passive at home. In some ways, I was following in the footsteps of my father. I was having an affair…not with another woman, but with Jesus' bride—the church. In the Bible, the church is often referred to as the *bride* of Christ. Ministry at church had become my first priority, and as a result I was missing my more important calling as the leader of my family.

In the summer of 2003, God brought me to a place of repentance and brokenness. I had to confess that I was a hollow man. I looked good on the outside, but behind the scenes I was not walking spiritually with my wife and children. God was merciful to me. It is never too late to repent and ask God to change your heart! By His grace, God has been increasingly turning my heart to Him, to His Word, to Amy, and to our children.

The Journey Ahead

Our relationship with Christ and with each other has changed dramatically in our fifteen years together. In the pages ahead we will share more of our story with you. We hope it is obvious we did not decide to write a book on Christian marriage because we have it all figured out. But we have become convinced God has it all figured out, and He has revealed His plan and purpose for marriage and family in the Bible. We are praying God will use this book, specifically the words that come from His Word, to transform your relationship into a visionary marriage.

We pray that the words that follow will align with the eternal truth of God's Word, and accomplish great things in your heart and life. Let everything that comes from human wisdom or understanding fall away.

For His Glory,
Rob and Amy Rienow

Introduction

If I profess with the loudest voice and clearest exposition every portion of the truth of God except precisely that point which the world and the devil are at that moment attacking, I am not confessing Christ, however boldly I may be professing him. Where the battle rages, there the loyalty of the soldier is proved, and to be steady on all the battlefield besides is mere flight and disgrace if he flinches at that point.[1]

Martin Luther

Christian marriage is under assault in our world today. If you want to truly pursue the marriage God has for you, be prepared for resistance. You will have to push back on the shallow vision of marriage that comes from the culture around you, from your family background, and maybe even from your Christian friends. It will not be easy...but it will be worth it.

Visionary Marriage is not...

This is not a book about secrets, tips, and tricks to building a more enjoyable relationship. You won't find chapters on improving your communication, finances, or your sex life. These things are important, but you probably already have excellent books on your shelves which can help in those areas.

You also won't find a lot of heartwarming stories and anecdotes. Throughout the book, we share many highs and lows from our personal journey, but *our* story isn't the point. While hearing the ups and downs in other marriages can be helpful, we don't believe that our story, or any other family's story, has the power to transform *your* marriage.

This is also not intended to give a comprehensive picture of Christian marriage, or a book designed for couples in serious crisis. We have walked alongside couples going through the most serious of situations—from adultery, to violence, to addiction. God has restored and healed some of these relationships while others have ended in divorce. We take these issues seriously. This book is not designed to provide an intervention plan for these kinds of marital crises. However, *Visionary Marriage* will provide you with a blueprint which may help you during these challenging times.

We will take an extraordinary journey through the wisdom God has revealed in the Bible to guide and direct us in our roles as husbands and wives, but in many areas we will only be able to scratch the surface.

Visionary Marriage will not be an easy read. If you go down this road, and you are ready to hear from God through what He has revealed in Scripture, you will be challenged. God may call you to change your priorities, your opinions, and your life purpose.

Visionary Marriage is…

We want to help you capture a God-sized vision for your marriage and for your family. Our focus will be on the big-picture purpose for marriage, not more things to add to your relationship to-do list. Does your marriage have a purpose? If so, where did that purpose come from?

The truth is if we don't know the purpose for something, we have little or no hope of being successful with it. But where can we hope to discover the purpose for our marriage and family? The purpose for something is determined by its creator. Because marriage was created by God, He alone defines its purpose.

It is important for you to know up front, we will do our best to approach every issue from a Christian perspective. That means we believe God has revealed everything we need to know about life, marriage, family, and children in the pages of the Bible. Both of us accepted Christ when we were children. As we grew up, we became convinced the Bible was unlike any other book…that it was divinely inspired, and completely true. However, even though we believed the Bible was true, we did not understand that it was also *sufficient*. This will be a recurring theme in the pages ahead. To believe the Bible is sufficient is to believe that not only is it completely true, but that it is enough to shape our thoughts, perspectives, and opinions on every important issue of faith and life.

In the Christian world, you won't get much push-back if you want to stand on the truth of the Bible. However, it is another matter to claim that the Bible is all you need to determine truth. We enter particularly dangerous territory when we claim the essential foundations for marriage, parenting, and the roles of husbands and wives are revealed by God in the pages of Scripture. That is where we seek to stand, and we pray you will join us for the glory of God! God's purpose for your marriage may surprise you. We guarantee it will challenge you.

Before you start the first chapter, take a moment to pray. Pray for God to do something special in your marriage and in your family. Ask Him to prepare your heart to grow, and to give you the grace to be the husband or wife He created you to be.

To believe that the Bible is sufficient is to believe that not only is it completely true, but that it is enough to shape our thoughts, perspectives, and opinions on every important issue of faith and life.

CHAPTER 1

Why Marriage?

Turn back the clock

Do you remember getting engaged, preparing for your wedding, and celebrating your wedding day? For some it was only a few months ago, for others decades. Think back to that time and consider this question. *Why* did you get married?

We have asked many engaged couples this same question, "Why are you getting married?" Here are some of the classic answers:

"She is my best friend."

It sounds so sweet, doesn't it? But is being best friends enough on which to build a marriage? There will be a day when you don't feel like best friends. There will even be days when you don't like each other. What then?

"He makes me laugh."

Laughter is a blessing in a relationship, but it is not a sufficient reason to get married. Every couple experiences hard times when no one is laughing.

"We are getting married because we make each other happy."

It is true that happiness is part of God's plan for marriage. In Deuteronomy 24:5 God says that a man is not to have any additional responsibilities put upon him during his first year of marriage so that "he is to be free to stay at home and bring happiness to the wife he has married." Happiness is a blessing, but in the end is happiness what marriage is all about? God created marriage for far greater purposes than our personal happiness.

"She completes me."

How many romantic movies have used this line? Despite the fact it is overused, there is some substance behind this answer. God created the man Adam in the Garden of Eden, and in Genesis 2:18 the LORD said, "It is not good for the man to be alone. I will make a helper suitable for him." There is a sense in which Eve completed Adam. But was this the grand purpose for which God blessed them with the gift of marriage?

Is There Any Difference?

We have had the opportunity to walk the path of engagement with many couples through our counseling ministry at church. The majority of these couples have been followers of Jesus Christ. Yet, when asked, "Why are you getting married?" they gave answers which *any* couple could give! Rarely have we heard engaged Christian couples give a distinctively Christian, Bible-driven, Gospel-centered reason for why they were getting married.

Instead, we have often bought into the world's short-sighted, half-hearted, self-centered vision of what marriage is all about. We throw a little church and Jesus into the mix and come away believing that we have a Christian marriage.

Thankfully, God has raised up many Christian ministries which have impacted countless marriages, including our own. As a young Christian couple, we were blessed by both marriage books and seminars which helped us improve our marriage in many ways. As a result of these ministries, we learned to communicate better, manage our money more effectively, and enjoy a better sex life. All of these things are important. Yet, the end result for us was an increased focus on our own personal happiness, while we were missing God's grand purpose for our marriage.

Your marriage today

A moment ago you turned back the clock to consider the question, "Why did you get married?" Here is another question, "*Why are you still married?*"

The way we answer these questions determines, in large part, the success of our marriages. These "*why*" questions are purpose questions. They are mission questions. Many, if not most, Christian couples get married without a clear Christian purpose for their family. We were definitely in this category when we were married in 1994. We were ignorant of what a Bible-driven, Christ-exalting, Gospel-expanding marriage was all about. We weren't stupid, just ignorant. We did not know, and despite graduate degrees from Christian colleges, we had not been taught all that God had said in the Scriptures about His purposes and plans for marriage and family.

We were oblivious to the fact that many of our views about marriage, family, and children had been derived from secular culture instead of God's Word. We had studied and considered what the Bible said about the church, evangelism, worship, missions, money, morality, salvation, the end times, heaven and hell. But we had little to no theological understanding of God's purposes for the family. Amazing! God created the family as the fundamental institution upon which all human life and civilization rest, and yet we never gave it serious theological thought.

> **We were ignorant of what a Bible-driven, Christ-exalting, Gospel-expanding marriage was all about.**

It is our prayer that through the Scriptures we will explore in *Visionary Marriage* that God will give you passionate, compelling, unifying mission and purpose for your family!

A house with no foundation

Getting married without a Christ-centered, Bible-driven purpose is like building a house without a foundation. It can be done. You can purchase a plot of ground, and pay someone to start building a house right there on the grass. The frame will go up, and the roof will go on. The electrical, plumbing, drywall, fixtures and appliances can all be installed. You can move right in.

For the first few days, even months, life is great. The new house is everything you hoped for. Then you notice a big crack in the wall. The next day the roof starts leaking. A storm comes and the carpets are sopping wet. Why did all these things happen? Did the wall crack because of bad drywall? Did the roof leak because of defective shingles? Did the carpet get wet because of poor installation? All these problems arose for the same reason—a faulty foundation.

This is how we began our married life. Sure, we did some premarital counseling, and it was helpful. The mentors that helped us loved the Lord and loved us. But the relationship issues that we tried to work on were all above the ground. We talked about communication, finances, sexuality, and in-laws. In fact, when we first began our marriage ministry together, these were the subjects we thought were the most important things that young couples needed to talk about. Sadly, all our attention went to "building the house" rather than laying the foundation.

As a result, after ten years of marriage, we realized we didn't just have communication problems, we had foundation problems. Our marriage had far deeper issues than we realized, because we had entered into our marriage with our own ideas about what family was all about rather than God's purpose for family as revealed in the Bible.

This is not to say that if a couple does not build with a biblical foundation they are doomed to misery and divorce. Many couples, Christians and non-Christians alike, are able to keep patching the holes and fixing the leaks. They stick together and many blessings come from their faithfulness to one another. But far too many of us settle for a good marriage. God has an extraordinary purpose and plan for your marriage! He has revealed it in the pages of Scripture for those that will read it, believe it, and seek to obey it.

Repairing the foundation

Imagine discovering that your home has a foundation problem. The only way to fix it is to do the messy work of ripping out flooring and digging down around the house to make the needed repairs. God had to lead us through that messy work. It was serious, and it was hard.

God had to turn our hearts first to Him, then to His Word as a sufficient guide for our family. We will share with you how God brought us to a place of repentance and how He has started the process of replacing our everyday marriage, with a visionary marriage. We are praying He will do the same for you.

Prayer:

Dear God,

Thank You for my marriage. With all of our joys, and with all of our problems, thank You. I don't want to build our marriage without a foundation. I realize there may be major areas of my mind, heart, and life You need to change before I can be the husband/wife You created me to be. I realize that examining the foundation of our marriage may be messy. Free me from fear. Open my heart, and the heart of my husband/wife, to Your purpose for our family.

In Jesus' name, Amen.

Questions for further thought and discussion

1. In your opinion, what is the main reason why couples choose to get married?

2. In your opinion, what are some of the differences, if any, that you have observed between Christian marriages and non-Christian marriages?

3. Think back to when you were engaged. What was one attitude, belief, or expectation you had about marriage that you now realize was incorrect?

CHAPTER 2

The Power
of Purpose

In the last chapter, we encouraged you to turn back the clock and ask yourself, "Why did I get married?" Then we brought the same question into the here and now, "Why am I still married?" The way you answered those questions forms the default mission statement for your marriage and family.

Are we compatible?

One of the most common, but flawed reasons people get married is because they feel they are "compatible." Couples are even encouraged to live together in order to discover this mystery of relationship compatibility. Tragically, 80% of couples who live together before they get married end up in divorce court. How can this be true? Wouldn't couples who live together before marriage discover problems in the relationship and call things off? Rather than weed out bad relationships, living together frequently perpetuates them. The couple who lives together before marriage is under the illusion that they are truly getting to know each other. After all, they see each other at their worst, smell each other at their worst, and have to deal with the day-to-day annoyances of sharing space with someone.

The truth is they are still putting their best foot forward in the relationship. Then they get married, and the real man and real woman emerges. Marriage intensifies everything. The good in the relationship gets better. The bad gets worse. Six months into the marriage she says to him, "You changed. I don't know what happened to us. Things were so much better before we got married..."

The virtue and value of living together before marriage is a lie from the world designed to destroy relationships. A companion lie is that a couple needs to find out if they are sexually compatible with one another. Many who hold this view will say, "You wouldn't buy a car without a test drive would you?" This is an easy one to answer. If you are a male, and you are engaged to a female, or vice versa, you are sexually compatible. The parts will fit. God figured out all that stuff ahead of time. Using the gift of sexuality before you are married will damage your sexual future together, not improve it.

The best sexual relationship is built on a healthy emotional and spiritual relationship. Can two strangers hook up for some temporary pleasure? Sure. But don't confuse that with great sex, or a rush of feelings with relational compatibility.

Don't Ever Change

Are you a different person than you were five years ago? Have you matured? Have some of your convictions and beliefs changed? Do you have different hobbies and interests? For some of us, thinking of who we were five years ago makes us cringe! For some reason, many couples think that the person they are marrying is going to "freeze" exactly as they are for the next 75 years. They think he or she is going to look the same, act the same, and feel the same from now until eternity. This is a recipe for disaster.

Amy's dad gave her wise advice when she was dealing with a difficult dating relationship in college. He said, "You think you know this man, but you don't. You think you know yourself, but you don't." He understood this principle that we are not snapshots in time, but always changing and growing.

When you say "I do" you are making a lifetime commitment to a moving target. In the past five years, you have changed dramatically; physically, emotionally, and spiritually. You are going to change dramatically in the next five years. The same is true for your spouse. The spirit behind Christian wedding vows is, "I am with you no matter what. No matter how you change and grow. No matter how I change and grow. I choose to be with you."

When you say "I do" you are making a lifetime commitment to a moving target.

If we are always changing, what hope does that give us for a stable relationship? Is there anything truly solid upon which we can build a family?

The Right Purpose

Knowing the purpose for something is vital. Why would you ever get a job? You work to provide for yourself and for your family. You need clothes, food, shelter, etc. If you want these things, you need to work. So you show up for the first day at your new job. Unfortunately, the person who works in the cubicle next to you chews gum too loudly. So, you march right into the boss' office and quit. You tell the boss in no uncertain terms, "I am not going to put up with this sort of rudeness. I am out of here!" Thankfully, this is not the way people function in the workplace. Why? Because we understand that we are going to work for the purpose of providing for ourselves and our families, not to become life-long best friends with every co-worker. Having a clear sense of purpose enables us to deal with hard times, annoyances, and problems. In the same way, when we understand and embrace a clear purpose for our marriage and family, we have the strength to face hard times.

But having a clear purpose is not enough. We need to have the *right* purpose. If we think the purpose of a cell phone is to hammer nails, not only will we hammer nails very poorly, but we will totally miss out on what the cell phone can really do for us. If we think marriage is all about our personal happiness, we will fail to experience God's true purpose for us. If we think marriage is about companionship, our deepest desires for friendship will not be satisfied, and at the same time we will miss the compelling mission God has for us.

So what is the true purpose for marriage and the family? How would you answer that question? Why did God create marriage?

While we may have our ideas about what marriage is all about, God alone has the right to answer this question. Marriage is not a human idea. Males and females did not emerge from the primordial soup, or swing down from the trees and conjure up some sort of social contract which we now refer to as marriage. God made Adam, and quickly spoke the truth that it was not good for man to be alone (amen). God quickly put him to sleep, and created Eve from his rib. Adam didn't have anything to do with it. Eve didn't have anything to do with it. The gift of marriage, sex, and children were all created, and designed by God. He created the institution of the family with a purpose.

In the pages ahead, we will walk through the Bible and discover that God created marriage for two overarching purposes, 1) the spiritual transformation of one another, and 2) raising godly children.

Know Your Role

When our purpose for marriage is God's purpose for marriage, an everyday marriage turns toward becoming a visionary marriage. In order to understand God's purpose for marriage, we need to examine what God has said about the purpose and role of the husband, and the purpose and role of the wife. If we are not clear about our purpose as individual men and women, we can't be clear about our purpose together.

On a basketball team, the point guard needs to understand how to play his position, the center—his position, etc. When all the players know their roles, then the team can best accomplish their shared mission. Within a company, each employee has to be clear about their responsibilities. Managers need to manage. Sales people need to sell. Accountants need to keep the books in order. When each person in the company excels in their individual role, the mission of the company has the best chance of success.

From the very beginning, in Genesis chapter one, God created men and women with equal value, worth, dignity, and importance. God also chose to create men and women differently so they might fulfill different roles and purposes in the family. The first step toward a visionary marriage is for the husband and the wife to understand these roles. When each partner in the marriage knows their role, then they are ready to enter into a shared mission together. In the pages ahead, we will explore the clear texts in the Bible where God gives husbands and wives their own distinct calling and job descriptions, and then expand our vision to see God's amazing plan to unite husband and wife in a single mission for the glory of God.

> **When each partner in the marriage knows their role, then they are ready to enter into a shared mission together.**

Danger Ahead

If you choose to move on to the next chapter, you are taking a big risk. You risk exposing your heart, mind, marriage and family to the unchanging truth God has given us in the Bible. We have become convinced that the Bible is not only completely true, but it is completely sufficient. We believe it is enough to shape our thoughts and opinions on every important issue. God has spoken clearly in the Bible about His calling and purpose for husbands and fathers. God has spoken clearly in the Bible about His calling and purpose for wives and mothers. We have to decide if we will accept it as the truth. We have to decide if what God has revealed in Scripture will be enough for us.

Perhaps you are unsure about the reliability of the Bible. We are glad you are taking the journey of visionary marriage with us. Be encouraged. God is there. He loves you. He wants to reveal Himself to you, and show you His purpose for your marriage and life together. If God really does have a purpose for your marriage, wouldn't you want to know what it is? Take a chance. Be open to the possibility that the Bible really is what it claims to be—the words of God.

We pray that when you complete this journey, and you consider the question, "Why are we still married?" that you will say:

We are married because we are Christians, and we believe God has called us to be married, so we might help each other become more like Christ, and we might have the opportunity to impress the hearts of our children with a love for God. God has given us a shared mission of equipping the next generation to make a difference in this world for Christ, and that they in turn would raise our grandchildren to know and love God. We remain committed to one another because we believe God wants to use our marriage to glorify Himself and to launch a massive multi-generational ministry that would shine for Christ in our neighborhood, our church, our nation, and to the ends of the earth.

Prayer:

Dear God,

I want to know why You created marriage and the family. The world is filled with lies, and I confess that it is easy for me to believe those lies, or mix those lies in with Your truth. Give me the courage not just to read, but to believe what You have said in the Bible about the roles of men and women in marriage and parenting. I want to know the truth, and I want to live it out.

In Jesus' name, Amen.

Questions for further thought and discussion

1. In your opinion, why is the divorce rate so high?

2. Does your understanding of your marriage change when you realize that your spouse and you are both "moving targets?" If so, how?

3. When someone says, "We need to look in the Bible in order to understand the role of men and women in marriage and family," people frequently become uncomfortable. Why do you think this is?

| *Visionary Marriage*

CHAPTER 3

Love

If I wanted to find out whether a man was a Christian, I wouldn't go to his minister. I would go and ask his wife. I tell you, we want more home piety just now. If a man doesn't treat his wife right, I don't want to hear him talk about Christianity.[2]

D.L. Moody

Before we begin, I (Rob) want to encourage wives to carefully read and understand these chapters about men becoming Christian husbands. You cannot encourage your husband to become the man God created him to be, if you are not clear yourself about what a godly man is and does. Your mission as a wife is not to help him become the husband and father you want him to be, but rather the husband and father God wants him to be.

Who Needs a Job Description?

Men, imagine you have been working at the same job, with the same company for ten years. Things are going well. You have respect inside and outside the company. Job security isn't a concern, and the bills are getting paid. It's Monday morning, and you show up for another week of work. You sit down at your desk, and as is your habit each morning, you open your top drawer and pull out your job description. Each morning, you go over the points and sub-points, making absolutely sure you know what you should be doing that day. After all, you would not want to make any critical errors. Reviewing your job description each morning helps you stay on track.

Do any of us do this when we get to work in the morning? No! Why not? Because we know what needs to be done. We understand our jobs, and we don't need a daily review of our job description. For most of us, that piece of paper comes out once a year at review time.

We don't need to review our job descriptions because we already have a clear understanding of what it takes to be successful at our jobs, and what our supervisors expect. But what if you had to take a new job you had never done before, with a new company you knew nothing about, and with no interview process where you could get additional information? They just told you to show up and get to work. In that case, you would be desperate to get your hands on that job description.

The latter scenario is the way it is for most men when we become husbands and fathers. Being a husband and father are the most important jobs we will ever do, and yet most of us simply dive into the deep end without ever having taken a "swimming lesson." We must know our job description backwards and forwards. We must have a clear, compelling vision and understanding of what God, our Creator, is calling us to be and do.

I did not have a father who coached me and trained me about how to be a godly husband and father. Nor did he give me a godly example to follow. As I have surveyed men at conferences around the country, I have found that less than twenty-five percent of Christian husbands report that their fathers understood and tried to practice the biblical roles for men in the home. Less than one percent reports their father did his best to thoroughly train him for the mission of being a Christian husband and father.

While we may not need to review our job description at work, we are in desperate need of reviewing our job description at home. If we want to be successful visionary husbands, we need to know what "the Boss'" expectations are for us. We need to know what being a husband is all about. Thankfully, God, who created the roles of husband and father, has given us a clear job description in the Bible.

God's Call to Husbands

I believe the primary job description for husbands in the Bible can be found in Ephesians 5:25-26.

> *"Husbands, love your wives, just as Christ loved the church and gave himself up for her to make her holy, cleansing her by the washing with water through the word..."*

I appreciate how God gets right to the point. It is not something I am proud of, but there are times in my relationship with Amy that I become impatient for her to get to the point in a conversation. Land the plane, Honey. I am particularly bad at this when we are talking on the phone. This is a fairly common male characteristic. We like to get to the point. Keep extraneous stuff to a minimum and just tell me what I need to know. God made men and He knows how we work. So, He gets right to the point. In just two verses, God encapsulates the overarching mission for husbands, and does so with three clear purpose-statements.

Purpose #1: Love your wife

One of the ways that the enemy attacks Christianity is to accuse the Bible of teaching male dominance and female subservience. Some go so far as to say that the Bible is abusive to women. This is absurd on every front. For starters, get out your history book and look at what has happened to the value and dignity of women in every country where Christianity has taken root. The more Christian a culture becomes, the more women are honored, blessed, liberated, cherished, and protected.[3]

Look at how clear God is about how we as husbands are to treat our wives. What is the first command He gives a husband? What is your first role? *Love* your wife.

Unfortunately, our culture has robbed us of biblical understanding of what it means to love someone. Love has become synonymous with "the warm fuzzies," lust, or some combination of the two. So people talk about falling in love (ie, getting a lot of warm fuzzies and you can't keep your hands off each other), and falling out of love (ie, losing the warm fuzzies, and the person's touch is revolting to you). When most people use the word *love*, they should really be using the word *like*. In marriage, there are times that we really like each other, and other times when we don't like each other at all. Feelings of *like* rise and fall in any relationship, because we treat each other in extremely kind and extremely unkind ways as we move through our lives.

Love has become synonymous with "the warm fuzzies," lust, or some combination of the two. The first bullet on your job description, your first purpose according to God is to *love* your wife. In the Greek language there are three primary words which are often translated into English as *love*.

The word *eros* described the passionate, physical, and sexual expression of affection between two people. *Phileo* was the word used to express companionship, friendship, and the enjoyment we feel when we are together with people with whom we share common interests and values. *Agape* was the word for committed, self-sacrificing love that gives preference to others. As you might expect, when Paul instructs a husband to love his wife as Christ loves the church, he uses the last of those three Greek words. [4]

God gives us a full definition of what this *agape* love is all about in 1 Corinthians 13:4-7.

"Love is patient, love is kind. It does not envy, it does not boast, it is not proud. It is not rude, it is not self-seeking, it is not easily angered, it keeps no record of wrongs. Love does not delight in evil but rejoices with the truth. It always protects, always trusts, always hopes, always perseveres."

Loving someone is a commitment of action and attitude. It is not an overused cliché to say that love is a choice. In my desk drawer at work I have a card that reads:

"When it comes to Amy I am patient. When it comes to Amy I am kind. I don't envy her. I don't boast around her. I am not proud with her. I am not rude to her. I don't try and get what I want and I am not easily angered. I keep no record of the wrong things she has done. I don't delight when bad things happen to her and I do rejoice when good things happen to her. I always protect her, always trust her, always hope in her, and I never tire of doing any of these things."

Is what I have written on that card a true and accurate description of how I love Amy? I wish it was. Unfortunately, I fall short of this every day. But it is a powerful daily reminder to me that *if* I tell my wife I love her, *this* is what I am saying, because this is what love is, according to God.

This card is also a daily reminder to me that if I want to love Amy (and I do), that I do not have the strength of will or the nobility of character to pull it off. This mission to be a godly husband is not something I naturally have in me. I struggle with too much sin, and my character is too broken to succeed. This drives me to my knees, and keeps me desperately seeking the power of the Holy Spirit to transform my character, and enable me to love Amy the same way the risen Christ loves the church.

Do you feel the same way? Are you clear in your own heart and mind that the bar God is calling you to get over cannot be cleared without supernatural transformation? If you think you have it in you to be a godly husband, either you don't know what God desires, or you have set the bar way too low.

Growing in Love

Look again at the list of actions and attitudes that comprise true love. There are seven positive (do) elements, such as being patient. There are eight negative (do not) elements, such as not being easily angered. True love is as much about what we do, as what we do not do. As you read them, identify which aspects of love God has enabled you to be most skilled, and which aspects you most need to grow.

• Patience
• Kindness
• Not envying
• Not boasting
• Not being arrogant
• Not being rude
• Not seeking what you want
• Not being easily angered
• Not keeping track of the wrong things your wife has done
• Not delighting in evil and suffering
• Rejoicing with truth and blessing
• Protecting
• Trusting
• Hoping
• Persevering

The more you do these things, the more you love your wife. The less you do these things the less you love your wife. Your feelings are not the measurement of your love. Your daily actions and attitudes are. I struggle with a lot of these, but patience would probably be at the top of the list. This character flaw in me is exacerbated when I am multi-tasking. If I am trying to check my email, help clean the kitchen, watch the kids, and keep an eye on the news, I am frequently impatient with Amy. My impatience then can become rudeness.

One area where God has blessed Amy and me as we seek true love in our relationship is "not keeping a record of wrongs." My mother, from as early as I can remember, taught me to practice Ephesians 4:26, "In your anger, do not sin: do not let the sun go down while you are still angry." Mom never let me and my brother go to bed without resolving any conflict we may have had during the day, and asking for each other's forgiveness. There have been many times in my fifteen years of marriage where Amy or I wanted to hang on to our anger from the day. The forces of evil love to tempt us to roll to the far side of the bed, turn our back on our spouse, and harden our hearts. Obeying this Scripture has required some late nights of conversation, honesty, tears, and repentance.

For a serious challenge, ask your wife to share with you the three things on God's love list that you do best, and the three in which she feels you need more growth. Thank her for her honesty and encouragement, and then listen carefully to her concerns.

In the next chapter, we will dig into the second purpose God has for husbands as revealed in Ephesians 5:25-26.

A Husband's Prayer for Himself

Dear God,

Thank You that I don't have to figure out what it means to be a good and godly husband. You have given me a clear job description in Your Word. I know my first purpose is to love my wife, but when I look at what that means, I realize I don't have it in me. I don't have the character, discipline, or skill to love my wife the way I should. Please empower me with Holy Spirit to make me the man I cannot be on my own. Help me to show my love for You, by loving my wife.

In Jesus' name, Amen.

A Wife's Prayer for Her Husband

Dear God,

Thank You for my husband. Thank You that You are at work in his heart, life, and character. Please bless him. Continue to build his character and encourage him. Convict his heart so he will believe Your Word in every area of his life. Thank You for the attitudes and attributes of love which my husband does well. Transform his heart to grow in the areas where he is weak. Use me to encourage him and bless him.

In Jesus' name, Amen.

Questions for further thought and discussion

1. Why do you think the world's definition of love, and God's definition of love are so different?

2. Love does not keep a record of wrongs. However, every married couple does things that are wrong, and therefore they hurt one another. What does forgiveness look like in your marriage?

3. Men, if you had to pick just one biblical aspect of love in which God would have you grow in this year, what would it be?

4. Women, how could you lovingly encourage your husband to become a better lover? In other words, in which of the characteristics of love from 1 Corinthians chapter 13 would God most want for you to help him grow?

CHAPTER 4

Serve

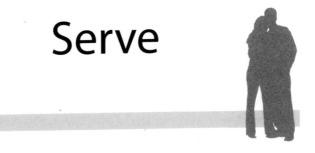

Husbands, love your wives, just as Christ loved the church and gave himself up for her to make her holy, cleansing her by the washing with water through the word...

EPHESIANS 5:25-26

In the last chapter, we looked at the first purpose that God gives to husbands: to love our wives. But it doesn't end there. God gives the husband his second mission and purpose in the next phrase from Ephesians 5:25; we are to give ourselves up for our wives. This is what Christ did for His bride, the church, and therefore this is what we are to do for our brides as well. To put it simply, God calls a husband to serve his wife.

Don't miss the theological connection that God makes between the mission of the husband and the work of Christ. God wants us to understand that how we treat our wives is a reflection of the gospel and of Christ Himself. When Christian men demand to be served, rather than serve, the gospel is perverted and Christ's work on the cross is obscured. In the same way, when Christian men are servants, and follow in the footsteps of Christ as they give themselves up for their wives, the gospel is visible and Christ is honored.

What is the husband's first purpose? To love. What is the husband's second purpose? To serve. This call to serve is far more than bringing your wife coffee in the morning. Although, I can personally attest this is an excellent idea. About a decade ago I heard that President George W. Bush brought his wife, Laura, coffee each morning. I figured, if the leader of the free world could fit that into his schedule, I could too. Small acts of kindness like this are the first things we usually think of when it comes to serving our wives. But please don't follow my example in this area. My tendency has been to think about things that I like and then do them for Amy, rather than think carefully and ask her what she would find most pleasing and helpful.

> **In the same way, when Christian men are servants, and follow in the footsteps of Christ as they give themselves up for their wives, the gospel is visible and Christ is honored.**

In recent years, God has been growing my character in the area of service. One of the ways God has helped me improve is by talking with Amy about where her *pressure points* are. Pressure points can be specific times of the day, or days of the week, which are particularly difficult for her. For instance, we have noticed that Thursdays tend to be emotionally exhausting days for us both. We are a few days into the week's demands, and we are both feeling a bit frayed. Pressure points can also be particular tasks, chores, or recurring problems. Maybe we are behind with the laundry, or the garbage seems to be continually overflowing. Perhaps there is a chronic discipline issue with the kids which needs additional focus. I am much more effective serving Amy when I ask her about her pressure points and then make a plan to specifically partner with her in those areas. My effort then creates the maximum positive impact for my wife and our home.

Serving by Protecting

Our call to serve our wives and "give ourselves up" for them may mean laying our lives on the line...literally. I frequently counsel couples who subscribe to what is often called an egalitarian view of marriage, where there are no God-defined roles for men and women. For the egalitarian, all roles are flexible and socially conditioned. When this touchy subject comes up I usually present the couple with a hypothetical scenario.

"I want you to imagine that you are lying in your bed at night. You both wake up with a jolt as you hear glass shattering out in the main area of the house. You hear heavy footsteps making their way toward the baby's room. Which one of you grabs the bat and goes out into the hall to protect the family?" Invariably, the woman immediately points at her husband and says, "Him!" At that point I say, "So you *do* believe that there are different roles for men and women in the family!"

One counseling situation was different. We were talking about roles in marriage, and after posing the situation above, I asked who would go take care of the bad guy. The wife said, "That's my job!" She seemed pleased with her self-aggrandizing pronouncement, while her husband slumped forward and put his head in his hands. He was ashamed and emasculated as his wife took pride in usurping his God-given role as the protector of his family.

There are many ways to fulfill this responsibility to protect our wives and children. We protect our wives and children when we drive according to the laws. We protect them when we double check that the doors are locked at night. We protect them with keeping sexual, violent, crass, and immature media out of our heads and out of our houses. If someone needs to run to the store late at night, husbands should do it.

Serving by Providing

With the rise of feminism in the culture and egalitarianism in the church, many couples today have lost a clear and noble vision for the husband to serve as the primary financial provider for the family. I have lost track of the number of Christian engaged couples we have seen who enter into marriage with two full-time incomes, and build their life (and their debt) based on those two salaries. They borrow money for houses, cars, and vacations based on their two-income, no kids, life stage. Both salaries are required to make all the monthly payments. Then God blesses them with a child! Their life mission and divine calling as a couple has now shifted into high gear. But who is going to take care of the baby? Who is going to be the keeper of the home? Who will pass faith and character to that child from day one? Someone else. Grandma. The babysitter. Daycare. Why? Because both full time jobs are needed to maintain the monthly debt payments.

We plead with engaged couples, and now with you, to pray with all your might and strategically work toward living off the husband's salary alone. If there is a period of time prior to children that the wife is working outside the home, put her salary toward savings or debt retirement. We know this is all easier said than done. Millions of couples are facing the reality that even basic needs cannot be covered with just the husband's salary. It is appropriate for both spouses to be working to meet a financial crisis. In addition, I know of many situations in which the husband has lost his job, and the wife's work is necessary to keep the family afloat. As we will learn later, the exemplary wife in Proverbs 31 works in the family business to aid in supporting the family. If this is your situation, my prayer is that the appropriate weight and pressure of the family's financial needs would rest squarely on the husband. When the wife is lying awake at night trying to figure out a way to make ends meet, while the husband sleeps peacefully, this vital role in the marriage has been inverted.

I have never met a wife and mother who *wanted* to have her husband depend upon her income in order to make ends meet. My prayer is that God will enable me to work hard and earn enough money to provide for our basic needs, and that any income that Amy may make would be additional funds that could go toward savings, special purchases, or debt reduction. Our purpose here is not to talk about who sits down with the bills each month and writes the checks. It may very well be that your wife is far more skilled with numbers than you are, and therefore it may make sense for her to manage the administration of the monthly finances. This is about who bears the ultimate responsibility for providing for the family.

I encourage you to test this principle. Men, here is how you can do it. Sit down with your fiancé or your wife and say something like this to her. "Honey, I have been thinking about our finances and our long-term goals. I think I have a great plan put together, and I want to share it with you. Here is my dream. Both of us work full time until we are 65-70 years old. We will have the kids in daycare from the time they are 2 months old, and then once they are in school, we can get them into one of those extended-day programs so we don't have to get babysitters after school. If we can pull this off, all of our family goals can be accomplished." Let me know what your wife thinks of your plan. I think I already know.

> **When the wife is lying awake at night trying to figure out a way to make ends meet, while the husband sleeps peacefully, this vital role in the marriage has been inverted.**

Perhaps it is your heart's desire for your family to function off of one income, and for the man to serve as the primary provider. But it isn't working out that way, and to be honest, there appears to be no light at the end of the tunnel. Two salaries aren't a luxury for you, they are a necessity. If that is your situation, I encourage you to face it head on. Pray. Pray hard. Pray often. Pray together. Get a tight reign on expenses. Be honest with each other about your feelings of fear and insecurity. Pray that God will provide a raise, a bonus, or a new job that will enable you to increasingly make the second income optional. Take a Christian financial planning class or seek out biblical financial counseling.[5] You are not doomed to the status quo, because God is real, and God answers prayer.

How Serving Fuels Your Romance

We started this chapter by talking about simple ways we serve our wives through small acts of kindness. For many couples, when they are dating or engaged, the relationship is filled with thoughtful gestures. A love note on her car. A flirting text to him while he is in class or at the office. Flowers…just because. Do you remember those days?

In marriage counseling, couples frequently tell me that their feelings for one another have changed. They go on to tell me the story of how when they were first married, they were so in love, and they felt so close. But as the years have passed, they grew more distant. Warmth was replaced with distraction. Distraction was replaced with irritation. I ask them to tell me about the positive things they are doing to show their commitment to one another.

"Are you going out on dates? Are you giving her flowers? Are you writing him encouragement notes? Are you bringing home gifts for no particular reason?"

"No."

"Why not?"

"We don't feel close and romantic toward one another anymore, so it is hard to do those things."

These couples have reversed cause and effect! They believe the reason they did all those acts of service and romance earlier in the relationship was because their feelings propelled them. They believe their feelings drove their behavior, but don't have the whole picture. Why did they feel closeness and warmth for one another? In part, because the relationship was filled with service and acts of kindness. The behaviors were driving the feelings, as well as feelings driving behaviors.

I am not saying that we serve our wives in order to manipulate their feelings. God calls us to serve our wives so that we might imitate Christ who gave Himself up for His church. But God built the marriage relationship in such as way that service fuels romance. One of the most discouraging things in the world for a husband is when he feels that his wife doesn't like him. Men, don't wait around for your wife's feelings to magically warm toward you. Warmth and closeness don't spontaneously emerge in any relationship. God built a woman's heart to respond to the love, service, and leadership of her husband.

A Husband's Prayer

Dear God,

Thank You for giving me a clear mission as a husband. I want to love my wife, and I want to serve her. I want to have the character and courage to give myself up for her. If it is ever required of me to sacrifice my life to protect my family, let me rise to the occasion. I feel the weight of responsibility to provide for my family. I give You all my fears and worries and ask You to make a way for my work to provide for all our family's financial needs. As I seek to serve my wife, let her feel cherished and valued.

In Jesus' name, Amen.

A Wife's Prayer for Her Husband

Dear God,

Thank You that You created my husband to be the protector of our family. Give him strength and courage for this task. I also know he feels pressure in a unique way to provide financially for our family. Bless the work of his hands. Expand his success. Show me everyday how I can help him become the husband, father, and man You created him to be.

In Jesus' name, Amen.

Questions for further thought and discussion

1. Men, can you think about some of the pressure points that your wife faces? How could you serve her in those areas?

2. Women, your husband bears a huge responsibility to protect your family in the face of danger. Do you thank him for this? How could you give him more affirmation in this area?

3. What is your financial vision as a couple? If you desire to have the husband serve as primary provider, do you have a plan to move in that direction?

4. What did you think of the final principle in this chapter that behaviors drive our feelings, rather than the common view that feelings drive our behaviors?

CHAPTER 5

Lead

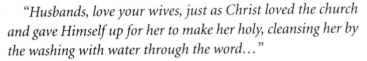

"Husbands, love your wives, just as Christ loved the church and gave Himself up for her to make her holy, cleansing her by the washing with water through the word…"

Ephesians 5:25-26

In the past two chapters we have considered the first two points in the Christian husband's job description. God calls a man to first love his wife, which means living and applying the actions and attitudes from 1 Corinthians 13. The second call is for a husband to serve his wife, giving himself up for her. God now turns our attention to the third and ultimate purpose for the Christian husband. It is this third purpose which separates the men from the boys, and everyday husbands from visionary husbands.

Look carefully at the Scripture from Ephesians 5 written above. A man is called to love and serve his wife for a particular reason. What is it? The reason is to make her holy. Have you ever wondered why God brought your wife into your life? Here is the answer. Your ultimate mission as a husband is to encourage and lead your wife to become more like Christ. God calls you to love her and serve her for a glorious purpose, that you might be God's instrument in shaping her into the woman that God created her to be. God has entrusted your wife's heart and soul into your care.

It overwhelms me, and frankly intimidates me, to think that God has entrusted Amy's soul to my care. God wants me to lead her and nurture faith in her? In many areas, she is more spiritually mature than I am. And yet, God's Word on this subject is plain for any man or woman who will read it and believe.

The husband's divine job description is clear: Love, serve, and lead. Not only is it clear, but it is precisely ordered. If you try to lead a woman, without first loving her and serving her... well, good luck with that! A woman's heart will likely not be led by a man who doesn't first love her and serve her. In fact, if a husband tries to lead his wife without first demonstrating his love for her and laying his life down for her, she will resent him. Leadership, no matter how good and right it may be, without a heart of love and sacrifice, will be received by the wife as domination and control. On the other hand, when a wife experiences love and service from her husband, she increasingly opens her heart to him, trusts him, and responds to his spiritual leadership.

Your ultimate mission as a husband is to encourage and lead your wife to become more like Christ.

Lead on!

A few chapters ago, we were brought face-to-face with the reality that we don't have it in us. God's call for us, as husbands, is a call beyond our character and competence. The call to lead our wives brings us to this same point. We can't lead our wives in a direction we are not going in ourselves. If I am not pursuing a deeper relationship with God and increased holiness in my private life, how can I nurture faith and holiness in Amy?

Did you ever play with dominoes when you were a kid? I could spend hours setting up a perfect track around the floor of my basement. Most of the time I would accidentally knock one over which would cause a chain

We can't lead our wives in a direction we are not going in ourselves.

reaction, ruining half my work! Once the track was perfectly set, with the smallest touch on the first domino, all the others would fall down.ieve that God lays out a series of interconnections in the Scriptures which function like those dominoes. Here they are:

Man—Marriage—Family—Church—Nation

Generally speaking, as the man goes, so goes the marriage. As the marriage goes, so goes the family. As the family goes, so goes the church. As the church goes, so goes the nation and the great commission. So if you were Satan and you wanted to destroy nations, churches, families, and marriages, what would you do? If you wanted to rob nations, churches, families, and marriages of spiritual vitality, Christian holiness, and Gospel-purpose, what would you do? You would do what Satan is doing in our world today; you would do all in your power to destroy and defeat men, because when men fall, the other dominoes fall as well.

Three Powerful Statements

To suggest that the husband has a leadership role in the marriage instantly causes tension. This flies in the face of everything our culture teaches. We will be wrestling with this issue in the chapters ahead. Here are three statements which we need to carefully consider. As a Christian, do you agree or disagree with this statement? "The head of every man is Christ."[6] If Jesus is the King of Kings and the Lord of Lords, then we should give a resounding, "Yes!" Now consider a second statement. Choose whether you agree or disagree. "The head of Christ is God." Our hope is that, again, you would affirm this. God the Father has authority over God the Son, even though they are both fully God.

Here is one last statement. Agree or disagree? "The head of a wife is her husband." This one feels more difficult, doesn't it? Consider how God spoke through the Apostle Paul on these three matters:

> But I want you to understand that the head of every man is Christ, the head of a wife is her husband, and the head of Christ is God.

1 CORINTHIANS 11:3 ESV

How can we affirm the first statement, "the head of every man is Christ," and the last statement, "the head of Christ is God," but deny the truth of one in the middle? We can't have the two, without the one. Husbands are called to loving, servant-leadership (love, serve, lead) in family life. It is his most important ministry and calling.

Passivity

In some ways, the opposite of spiritual leadership is spiritual passivity. I have been a part of two homes with passive husbands. In the home in which I grew up, my father did not take the lead role in the most vital areas of family life. The second home was my home, with me as the passive husband. For the first ten years of our marriage, I cared deeply about Amy and the kids, and I knew God had called me to lead, but I was giving my best energies elsewhere. I was actively engaged with my opportunities at work which was pleasing to God, but passive when it came to my responsibilities at home. Amy was like many other wives today. She wondered why I could be so dedicated, responsible, and visionary at work, but not using those same gifts at home.

My father and I were not the first men to struggle with passivity in the marriage relationship. In fact, we come by it quite honestly. It has been a struggle and a spiritual attack point from the beginning...the very beginning. After Adam and Eve had sinned, they covered their nakedness and sought to hide from God.

> But the LORD God called to the man and said to him, "Where are you?" And he said, "I heard the sound of you in the garden, and I was afraid, because I was naked, and I hid myself." He said, "Who told you that you were naked? Have you eaten of the tree of which I commanded you not to eat?" The man said, "The woman whom you gave to be with me, she gave me fruit of the tree, and I ate." Then the LORD God said to the woman, "What is this that you have done?" The woman said, "The serpent deceived me, and I ate."
>
> GENESIS 3:9-13 ESV

God first confronts Adam, because Adam was the spiritual head of the marriage relationship. He was the leader. At the end of the day, he was responsible for what happened. The apostle Paul affirms this in Romans 5:12 ESV, "Therefore, just as sin came into the world through one man, and death through sin, and so death spread to all men because all sinned..."

Adam's response to God's confrontation is classic. It is the ultimate example of blame, defensiveness, and deflection...three traits which I seem to have inherited from Adam as well. The first words out of Adam's mouth were, "The woman..." In other words, this was all her fault.

God first confronts Adam, because Adam was the spiritual head of the marriage relationship.

A few years ago we were packing the kids up in the car, preparing to head home from a fun afternoon at Grandma and Bop-bop's house. (Our oldest son called Amy's dad "Bop-bop" when he was learning to talk, and it stuck!) I was rushing around and went to load some stuff in the car. Without looking behind me, I threw open the back passenger door and squarely hit our then two-year-old daughter who had been quietly following behind me. The door hit her full force, and she fell back crying. Within a split second, I turned around, saw Amy standing about fifteen feet away and yelled, "What are you doing? Weren't you watching her?" Amy looked at me like I was crazy, which was an appropriate response. Amy had nothing to do with it. I wasn't paying attention and was totally responsible for what happened, yet my first response was to blame her…just like Adam blamed Eve.

Adam's first defense was "The woman…" Then Adam continues the sentence, "whom you gave to me." So first he blames Eve for his sin. Then he blames God for giving him Eve. Now it is God's fault! Eve followed suit. She didn't take responsibility for her sin either, but instead blamed the serpent.

Stepping Into Spiritual Leadership

Love, serve, and lead. That is God's call on my mission as a husband. Men, if you want to embrace this mission, you can count on Satan doing whatever he can to prevent your success. In my experience, he focuses the vast majority of his assault in this third area of spiritual leadership. Satan doesn't want you to love your wife, but he will tolerate it. He doesn't want you to serve her, protect her, and provide for her. He would prefer the opposite of all those things. But the enemy can live with you being a kind, hardworking, and even virtuous man…as long as you don't cross the line into your most important role of being the spiritual leader of your family. Nice, friendly marriages are no threat to what Satan has planned for your children and your church. You won't get too much resistance if you give yourself to loving and serving your wife. But if your ultimate mission is to encourage faith in her, if you try and engage with her spiritually through prayer, Bible reading, and Christian mission, prepare for the biggest and most important fight of your life!

Consider these four questions. Answer them in your mind as you read through them.

- In your opinion, do you think it is important to pray with your wife?
- Does God want you to pray with your wife?
- Is praying with your wife easy, compared to climbing Mount Everest? (In other words, is it easy or hard to bow your head, close your eyes, and say a few words to God while in the presence of your wife?)
- Do you struggle to pray faithfully with your wife?

I have asked thousands of men these four questions at our conferences. The overwhelming answers are, "Yes, yes, yes, and yes." They think it is important to pray with their wives. They believe God Himself wants them to do this. After thinking about it for a moment, they acknowledge that this is an easy thing to do. If you can talk, you can do it. Yet, despite the fact that it is important, God-ordained, and easy, men overwhelmingly report that they struggle in praying faithfully with their wives. How does this make any sense? The reason it *does* make sense is when you add the hidden part of the equation.

But the enemy can live with you being a kind, hard-working, and even virtuous man... as long as you don't cross the line into your most important role of being the spiritual leader of your family.

Prayer together is important. God does want you to do it. It is easy, *but the forces of evil throw everything at you to prevent you from doing it.* As a result, men struggle in this area of spiritual leadership. For most men, it isn't laziness, lack of desire, or distraction. It is spiritual battle. It is no accident that in Ephesians chapter 6 God reminds us, "For we do not wrestle against flesh and blood, but against the rulers, against the authorities, against the cosmic powers over this present darkness, against the spiritual forces of evil in the heavenly places." Ephesians 6:12 ESV

For the first twelve years of our marriage, I would give myself a D- grade in the area of taking the lead in praying with Amy. It was probably more like an F, but D- makes me feel a little better. As God began to turn my heart toward Amy, I increasingly fought through the awkwardness and spiritual resistance to pray with her. We began praying together each night before going to sleep. For a few years now, we have been praying faithfully together. I have many more years of failure than success, but we are moving in the right direction. It is never too late to repent and focus on the mission. You would think that praying together would be easy now, right? I wish that was true. Here is what happens to me, almost every night, as I get in bed. The Holy Spirit prompts me, "Rob, you should pray with Amy." Then the spiritual attack begins. I start feeling awkward, hesitant, and even a little embarrassed. Where could those feelings possibly come from? Is God making me feel that way? Obviously, not! Is Amy bristling at my attempts to pray with her? No. I am under spiritual attack! The last thing in the world that the forces of evil want is for me to embrace my mission as the spiritual leader in my marriage and in my home. If you want to step into spiritual leadership, you have to step into the battle. In the coming chapters, after Amy walks through the key Scripture passages dealing with God's job description for wives, we will talk in more practical terms about how to build a passionate, one-hearted, spiritual relationship.

Breakthrough

I remember a time when Amy and I were walking from home to church with our son RW. He was only three-years-old. As we approached the church, RW said, "Is this where you live, daddy?" I laughed at first…but later cried.

God truly turned my heart to Amy after 12 years of marriage. It wasn't that I didn't love her or wasn't committed to her. I did and I was. But my heart, passion, leadership, and vision were focused at work, rather than at home. My journey of repentance started a few years earlier. It began when God turned my heart to the ministry of my children. I had been serving as a full time youth pastor for eleven years, and my heart and mind were focused on passing my faith to these teenagers. When I was at work, I was thinking about work. When I was at home, I was thinking about work. I was all about these great spiritual *opportunities* while I was neglecting my spiritual *responsibilities.*

God had entrusted four children to my care. As a Christian, I knew it was my mission to "make disciples," but when I thought about that grand mission, I skipped right past the souls of my own children! God brought me to a place of deep brokenness and repentance. I asked Him to turn my heart to my children and give me the grace to impress their hearts with a love for God and help them get safely home to Him. Our family has never been the same. My work has never been the same either! As God turned my heart toward ministry at home, He blessed me with greater impact, joy, and effectiveness as a pastor.

I began waking up in the morning and instead of my first thoughts drifting toward checking my email, I had the front burner thought, "The spiritual growth of my children today is my responsibility. What's the plan?" God would also frequently bring this thought to my mind, "You should not expect anything out of your kids that you, as their father, are not intentionally investing into them." I expect my kids to be happy, pleasant, obedient, respectful and kind. I am not sure what happened, but my kids didn't come with those things pre-programmed. My children naturally gravitate toward sinfulness (like their dad). Yet, I expect these positive things, and more, out of them! Think about the absurdity of that for a moment. We expect things out of our kids that do not naturally reside in them. How unfair! Indeed it is unfair, if we as fathers don't make it our mis-

> **As a Christian, I knew it was my mission to "make disciples," but when I thought about that grand mission, I skipped right past the souls of my own children!**

sion to teach, train, nurture and invest these things into the hearts and minds of our children.

Needless to say, my relationship with my children was transformed, and our family was as well. Little did I know that God was preparing to take this repentance and transformation to an even deeper place. I was on our church's men's retreat.[7] After one of the sessions, God brought me to a place of deep repentance about my role as spiritual leader in my home. But this time it was not about my relationship with my children, it was about my relationship with Amy. I was cut to the heart, as I had to confess that I had not awakened a single day of my married life with the front-burner thought, "Amy's spiritual growth today is my responsibility. What's the plan?" Never had I considered the truth that I should not be expecting things out of Amy that I am not seeking to intentionally invest into her. It is not the same as with my children, but I do really like it when Amy is kind, loving, and respectful. These are things I "expect" out of her. Yet, what was I doing, the one God created to be her spiritual leader, to lovingly encourage these things in her? I had to confess that I had no plan or passion to help my wife grow in her faith and become the woman that God created her to be. I asked God to change me, and turn my heart to the ministry of my wife's soul. He did and He continues to help me every day in which I seek to be obedient and rely on Him.

The Journey Ahead

In the next few chapters, Amy will walk through the biblical calling for wives. If you thought that these chapters were challenging, buckle up! More than anything we want to be responsive and faithful to what God has said in His Word about His purposes for men and women in the home. We believe that the Scriptures alone are powerful and sufficient to transform our hearts, change our character, and shape our families. After the subsequent chapters focusing on God's job description for wives, we will shift our focus toward practical implementation of the vision and principles we have been learning. What does a visionary marriage look like in day-to-day life? But before we put the vision together, we need to consider the other side of the equation, what is God's purpose and call for wives?

Prayer (for husbands):

Dear God,

When I consider that my ultimate mission as a husband is to lovingly lead my wife to become more like Christ, I am overwhelmed. At least I understand a little of what it means to love and serve her. I am far from perfect in those areas, but it feels way out of my league to think of myself as the spiritual leader in our relationship. Do not let me forget that I am in a spiritual battle when it comes to my leadership in my family. Remind me to fight that spiritual battle with prayer and Scripture. Help me to believe Your Word, that my ministry to my wife's soul is my most important calling in the world. Turn my heart to my wife. Make it the greatest passion and focus of my life to encourage faith in her, so that one day I can present her back to You.

In Jesus' name, Amen.

Questions for further thought and discussion

1. Husbands, your biblical job description is three-fold: Love, serve, and lead...in that order. Which of these is the hardest for you to do? Why?

2. Wives, how does it make you feel to know that your husbands are under spiritual attack when it comes to their calling to be the spiritual leaders of the family? How would remembering this change your approach in regards to how you encourage him to engage spiritually at home?

3. Do you agree with the dominoes? Man, marriage, family, church, and nation? In what ways do you see these connected? Where might there be exceptions?

CHAPTER 6

A Bold
Question

God has a purpose for the Christian husband. Do you believe God has a purpose for the Christian wife? This is a difficult question. As women, most of us are eager to discuss the role of the husband in marriage. I (Amy) have met many women who feel their husbands are not the spiritual heads of their households. Most Christian women believe their husbands *should* be in this position, and desire their spiritual leadership. I have met few, if any, Christian women who do not believe their husbands *should* be the head of their marriage.

In Christian circles these two statements women can speak about with ease: 1) Christian men should be the spiritual leaders of the home and 2) Most Christian men are not spiritual leaders in the home.

If it is safe for us as women to discuss what Christian men should be doing in our homes, why is it difficult or almost impossible to discuss what Christian women should be doing in the home? Did God have a purpose for men in marriage but no purpose for women in marriage? Do women get to pick what their purpose will be? What is the purpose of the Christian wife? In our day, these are threatening questions indeed.

A while ago I was reading through a one-year devotional Bible for women. This Bible was set up like all one-year Bibles, with passages from the Old and New Testaments and selections from Psalms and Proverbs. Because this was a women's devotional Bible, there were several inspirational quotes from Christian women in the sidebars. There was also added to each day's reading a bold passage of Scripture. For example, Psalm 23 might begin with, **The Lord is my shepherd, I shall lack nothing,** but the rest of the passage would be in the regular font. These bolded verses were obviously the editor's way of directing the female reader to pay attention to these texts. Because it was a women's Bible, the editors were highlighting verses that they believed were important for women. When I was reading Ephesians, I thought it was interesting that, "However…the wife must respect her husband" (Eph. 5:33), was *not* in a bold font. It seemed that if the editors were trying to highlight verses that were important to women, surely this would be one of them. I then became curious. As I searched through the Bible, I realized that the most well-known verses that directly related to women were not bolded. Even Proverbs 31 was not bolded. It was odd to me that in a Bible marketed to women, passages directly relating to women were not highlighted.

Unfortunately, there is a lack of "boldness" today in addressing the mission of the Christian wife. It is not politically correct to talk about it. From my own experience, I remember that Rob and I did not have Ephesians 5, which contains direct instructions for both husbands and wives, read at our marriage ceremony because we believed it would be too controversial. We were both in graduate school at a Christian college and were well-educated in the egalitarian view of gender roles. We did not want to have something read at our wedding that may have been offensive to the non-Christians who were at the ceremony. We

> **Unfortunately, there is a lack of "boldness" today in addressing the mission of the Christian wife.**

were thinking evangelistically. It was better to stay away from the submission issue altogether than to somehow explain our position of mutual submission in a wedding ceremony.

This was the regard I had for the Ephesians 5 passage when I got married. Just as in our ceremony, it was relatively optional in my understanding of my new role as a wife. Because of Jesus' grace, my attitude is quite different now. I wish I had understood that Ephesians 5 gave me a central part of my job description as a Christian wife. Of course, this is not all of my God-given job description. In the chapters ahead, we will examine Ephesians 5:22-33, as well as passages from Genesis 1-2 and Titus 2. These are three primary texts in the Bible which address the bold question, "What is the purpose of the Christian wife?" We will examine each passage and pray that God, according to His grace, will teach us the purpose of the Christian wife as clearly as we understand the purpose of the Christian husband.

CHAPTER 7

Help

I can remember times when a pastor or Bible teacher asked me to turn to Genesis 1 and 2 and a boring sigh would release inside of me. I would think, "Come on already, hasn't this been covered enough?" I wanted to intellectually shut down because I wrongly felt that I had learned all there was to learn from those passages. Over the years, however, I have been amazed how I learn more from God's Word each time I hear it.

So as I am about to begin in Genesis to answer the bold question relating to the purpose of the Christian wife, I imagine hearing some readers give a big sigh of boredom. I feel your pain. How many times can you read about the creation of Adam and Eve and get anything new out of it? But in order to answer the question about the purpose of the Christian wife, we need to begin with the beginning. It is in these first two chapters of Genesis that God creates man, woman, and the institution of marriage.

In Genesis 1:26-28 we have the account of the sixth day of creation.

> *Then God said, "Let us make man in our image, after our likeness. And let them have dominion over the fish of the sea and over the birds of the heavens and over the livestock and over all the earth and over every creeping thing that creeps on the earth." So God created man in his own image, in the image of God he created him; male and female he created them.*

And God blessed them. And God said to them, "Be fruitful and multiply and fill the earth and subdue it and have dominion over the fish of the sea and over the birds of the heavens and over every living thing that moves on the earth."

GENESIS 1:26-28 ESV

God created man and woman in the image of God, male and female he created them. Here in Genesis 1 it all sounds similar for the man and the woman, doesn't it? They both are created in the image of God and they both receive the same command to be fruitful, multiply, subdue and have dominion over the earth. All things are equal. In Genesis 2, we find a more detailed account of the creation of the man and the woman.

Then the LORD God formed the man of dust from the ground and breathed into his nostrils the breath of life, and the man became a living creature. And the LORD God planted a garden in Eden, in the east, and there he put the man whom he had formed.

GENESIS 2:7-8 ESV

The LORD God took the man and put him in the garden of Eden to work it and keep it.

GENESIS 2:15 ESV

Adam was formed and he was different from the rest of the living creatures that God made. The Lord God took the man and put him in the Garden of Eden to work and to keep it. Adam was given a mission before Eve was even in the picture. In the next few verses God tells us how and why He made Eve.

Then the LORD God said, "It is not good that the man should be alone; I will make him a helper fit for him." Now out of the ground the LORD God had formed every beast of the field and every bird of the heavens and brought them to the man to see what he would call them. And whatever the man called every living creature, that was its name. The man gave names to all livestock and to the birds of the heavens and to every beast of the field. But for Adam there was not found a helper fit for him. So the LORD God caused a deep sleep to fall upon the man, and while he slept took one of his ribs and closed up its place with flesh. And the rib that the LORD God had taken from the man he made into a woman and brought her to the man.

GENESIS 2:18-22 ESV

Even before Adam was really getting into his work, God saw that it was *not good* for man to be alone and he needed a helper fit for him. Obviously, none of the birds of the air, beasts of the fields, livestock or any living creature was a helper fit for the man.

> **They both are created in the image of God and they both receive the same command to be fruitful, multiply, subdue and have dominion over the earth.**

God was right. It is not good for man to be alone. Did you know that unmarried men have statistically shorter life-spans than married men?[8] Almost every aspect of a man's life, physically, spiritually and emotionally are negatively impacted by remaining unattached.[9] As God stated at the beginning of creation, it is not good for a man to be alone. We find evidence of this truth even today.

> **Did you know that unmarried men have statistically shorter life-spans than married men?**

God tells us that He created Eve to be Adam's helper. This is a lot more complicated than Genesis 1, isn't it? Now we have the word "helper" and the fact that God created man first and then the woman. Woman was the only part of God's creation which He made from another living being. Eve was created from the rib of Adam. Woman was God's answer for a helper, fit for the man. Not only do we have the creation of the woman but also the creation of the institution of marriage and family.

> And the rib that the LORD God had taken from the man he made into a woman and brought her to the man. Then the man said, "This at last is bone of my bones and flesh of my flesh; she shall be called Woman, because she was taken out of Man." Therefore a man shall leave his father and his mother and hold fast to his wife, and they shall become one flesh.
>
> GENESIS 2:22-24 ESV

I am going to ask you to do something very difficult. To think about or discuss the role of the wife as a helper to her husband brings up a lot of complicated, emotional responses. We bring our experiences from our own families and our own marriages to the discussion table. Out of our experiences, we would all have examples to share about how we have been hurt by our fathers, mothers and husbands. Some of us would share horrible stories of abuse, and others would share wonderful stories of blessings. *Yet our experiences should not dictate our theology.* In order to examine the biblical model of marriage, we have to step away from our own emotional reactions and look with objective eyes. As Christians, we are faced with the choice of whether we will trust our own experiences or the Bible.

Yet our experiences should not dictate our theology. We must understand that the institution of marriage and the family is not man's idea but God's idea. God created it and there is no human power that can alter it. If God is the creator of marriage, we will surely be blessed by following His design.

The First Marriage

For some reason, whenever I had studied Genesis 1-2, I often looked at it as merely the creation of men and women but not the creation of husbands and wives as well. It is undoubtedly both. Here in this passage we see that God gives man a mission, and then gives him a wife who will help him in that mission. Before God created Eve, He set Adam to work. God gave Adam plenty of work to do before the fall occurred. It is important to note that work is God's idea and not the result of the fall. However, God sees that man needs a helper fit for him in accomplishing his work. The woman joins the man in his work, and then they are established as a family. They become one flesh. This is how God will accomplish His desire to fill the earth with worshippers of Him. A man will leave his father and mother and hold fast to his *wife* and they shall become one flesh.

Therefore, in the days of creation, God created the man, gave him work to do, and then gave him a woman to become his wife to help him do his work. Wow, that really is rather simple. How on earth has it become so complicated today?

Sin entered into the first marriage just as it infects our marriages today. Because of the sin of Adam and Eve, their perfect beginning would soon result in pain in work, pain in childbirth, and pain in death. There has never been a perfect human marriage because the very first one brought sin to the human race. Men do not make perfect husbands, and women do not make perfect wives. There will be pain in all of our marriages because we are sinful people. But does this mean that God's original plan for marriage is imperfect? I do not think so.

A Fit Helper

God created the wife to be a helper fit for the man. This was part of God's perfect plan for marriage. At the end of Genesis 2 we have the introduction of the word "wife" in place of the word "woman." Here we get the phrase, "man and wife." Did you realize that this phrase came directly from the Bible? In modern weddings, it is rare to be pronounced as "man and wife," but instead we use the phrase, "husband and wife." Yet "man" and "wife" were the words used when marriage was first instituted in the Scriptures.

We can conclude that a woman becomes a fit helper to a man when she becomes his wife. Eve did not have any time as a *woman* before she became a *wife*. The role of the wife is to be a helper fit for her husband. This does not mean that the role of all women is to be helpers to all men. Rather, it is the role of wives to help their husbands.

We may not like what it says, but that *is* what God's Word says. I have sat in several Christian classes where teachers argued that this was not really what was meant by this passage. Some Christians have argued that it is only because of the fall that wives are considered as helpers to their husbands.[10] They then argue that our job as Christians is to restore male and female relationships to a pre-fall condition. The Bible does not support this view. This would be considered an egalitarian interpretation of the text. For centuries of church history there was little confusion or debate about the meaning of Genesis 1 and 2. It has always been difficult to practice, but not difficult to understand. Whether we like it or not, the text is clear in Genesis that God's plan for a wife was to be a helper fit for her husband. If this was God's original pre-fall plan for the wife, should it be our plan for our marriages too? I believe the answer is yes.

A Helper in Training

When I was first married, I attended a workshop in our church for helping people become more organized. I still look for ways to become more organized! The presenter relayed a story about a woman whose husband was considering a divorce because he never had clean underwear in his drawer. As I sat at my discussion table with many women much older than I, we all began to shake our heads. I assumed we were all thinking the same thing until one woman leaned over and whispered in my ear, "I cannot imagine being so unorganized." I had to hide my disgust. I was shaking my head because I could not imagine being married to such a jerk…why doesn't he wash his own underwear? (And yes, I can imagine being so unorganized.)

I share this story with you because at the beginning of my marriage I was not thinking of my role as a helper fit for my husband. With all the priorities I had for a given day, I did not wake up and place at the top of the list, how can I help my husband today? Because we were in ministry together, it worked out that I did start assisting my husband regularly with the youth group. This was a great benefit to our marriage because it pushed me into being a fit helper. Rob and I found such great joy working together. We liked it so much that we were determined for me to work less as a therapist in order to pursue a ministry job at church. Thankfully, our plans were thwarted time and again. I now see this

> **With all the priorities I had for a given day, I did not wake up and place at the top of the list, how can I help my husband today?**

as God placing us on His path rather than our own. As we had children, it became clear that both of us working in church ministry would not be beneficial for our family. We were becoming increasingly convicted about discipling our own children. It was *essential* for me to be home to accomplish our joint mission.

The way I helped my husband dramatically changed. I was no longer in the spotlight with him "doing ministry." I could not take all the trips, help him with counseling appointments, or join him for speaking engagements. My help was now primarily behind the scenes, focusing on my most important ministry. It was very difficult to give up so many things that I enjoyed. After all, my gifts had been used in these areas at the church. Yet, the more I died to my own plans, the more I embraced God's plans for my marriage.

I found more peace and joy living God's way. My husband's success is my greatest success.

Previously, I had felt that I had to make something out of myself that was separate from my role as a wife. I needed to have my own career goals or have specific roles in my husband's ministry at church. Yet as we had more children, it became more and more difficult to keep my separate goals afloat. It was easy to feel bitter at times about what I was sacrificing in order to be home with the children. I often felt I was the only one making all the sacrifices. Although this was not true, it felt that way to me.

Wait a Minute

I hear in the back of my head many concerns now being raised. Does this mean that a wife is reduced to a housekeeper? Does this mean a wife cannot work and has to stay at home? If these questions are going through your mind, I would like to ask you to be patient. We will talk more about these questions in later chapters. Right now we are trying to answer the question, "What is the mission of the Christian wife?" The Bible teaches that the wife is to be a helper fit for her husband. You can choose if you want to believe it or not. The question is not whether or not the Bible teaches it; rather whether we will believe it. There are some who would say that because this is in the Old Testament, and particularly in the early chapters of Genesis, this principle doesn't apply today. But the New Testament contains passages which are even stronger. Consider what the apostle Paul wrote to the Corinthians.

For man was not made from woman, but woman from man. Neither was man created for woman, but woman for man. That is why a wife ought to have a symbol of authority on her head, because of the angels. Nevertheless, in the Lord woman is not independent of man nor man of woman; for as woman was made from man, so man is now born of woman.

1 CORINTHIANS 11:8-12 ESV

This is another example of God affirming the equality of husbands and wives while at the same time clarifying their different roles.

Another question we should address is, "Do our husbands have the responsibility to help us?" First, we need to be clear that God's Word gives different jobs to husbands and wives. They are different but equally difficult jobs. Your husband is called to love you and he is called to give up his life for you. He is called to serve you. You are called to help him. Which job description would you prefer to have? I do not see anyone getting off easy in this picture.

A Perfect Plan for Imperfect People

Thankfully, by the grace of God, I now see that God's original plan for marriage, like the rest of His creation is good, very good. The Scripture talks about the man and wife becoming one flesh. It is difficult to be one flesh with two different career paths, two different missions, or two separate bank accounts. Every business has one mission statement, not two. Yet many of us get married without a one-flesh mindset.

There is a difference between sharing your life with another person and becoming one flesh. I think it is possible to have a good marriage by sharing your life with another person. Many couples successfully compromise and submit to each other in order to help each other meet their own goals. This is the view of a good marriage that is given to us by the world. This model

It is difficult to be one flesh with two different career paths, two different missions, or two separate bank accounts.

is not a *bad* model for marriage, but it is not the *best* model. It is not the biblical model. It is difficult to step away from the vision of marriage that we have received from the world to get a bigger vision of a biblical marriage.

The world wants a woman to believe she is insignificant if she does not have separate life goals apart from her husband's, or if she is "reduced" to simply helping her husband. Unfortunately, throughout history some men have dominated their wives and viewed the term "helper" as synonymous with "slave." In many cultures even today women are viewed in this manner. When God created the wife as a helper, He did not create a second-class citizen. He created a co-worker. He created the wife with equal value, equal worth, and equal dignity to help with the mission of her husband.

Sadly, there are very difficult marriage situations which sometimes require women to take hard steps to protect themselves and their families. If you are in a dangerous or crisis situation, taking necessary steps to protect yourself and your children is a part of helping your husband become the man God created him to be. Rob and I have counseled couples with every kind of serious issue, and we understand that there are no quick fixes. As we said in the introduction, this is not a book for marriages in deep crisis. If that is your situation, we encourage you to meet with your pastor or a Christian counselor in your community. Don't wait. Get help today!

No woman *wants* to help a husband who views his wife as the one who is supposed to keep his home clean, the family fed, and him happy. If these are the priorities of the husband, the wife has a difficult job. She desires to be part of the mission, not a slave to her husband's self-centered desires. It is easy to see how the feminist movement became so prominent in Western culture, specifically the United States. In the late 1800s during the Industrial Revolution, the work lives for many men changed dramatically. Instead of staying home and working in a family enterprise, many men worked away from the home for many hours each day. For many of these men their time away from home meant their hearts left their homes too. It was now the wife's responsibility for the home, period. Eve was not supposed to work the garden by herself! Of course, women started pining for the man's work outside the home. It may seem a lot more glamorous to go out into the world and be acknowledged for your accomplishments than to serve quietly in the home.

When Christian men's hearts turn toward work in order to pursue goals entirely separate from their primary mission in the home, Christian women are left with the heavy weight of leading the family. In some ways, men and women face the same struggle. Will the man view his primary calling and most important responsibilities before God his work at home, or his work and interests away from home? Similarly, will the woman view her primary calling and most important responsibilities before God her work at home, or her work and interests away from home? Unless both spouses have their hearts fully engaged with the primary mission of home, both the marriage and family will not function with the blessing and joy that God intends.

> **Unless both spouses have their hearts fully engaged with the primary mission of home, both the marriage and family will not function with the blessing and joy that God intends.**

A Unique Helper

At this point, you may be thinking that being a fit helper for your husband means that you simply stay at home and clean the house! A biblical model of marriage is not "Leave it to Beaver." There are many ways that wives help their husbands, and not all marriages will look the same.

In my experience, helping Rob evolved from working with him in church ministry to supporting his church ministry, by keeping our home running well. But what really had to change in my marriage was my mindset. I needed to learn to ask myself the question on a regular basis, "How can I help Rob?" When I began fulfilling this important part of my job description, I became more fulfilled. As I eagerly desired to help him, he reciprocated by better serving me. I still struggle with asking him specifically how I can help him each day, because it is so easy to completely focus on my children's needs, which are ever before me. But by God's grace, I now view myself as a helper fit for my husband as part of my purpose as a Christian wife. I hope to continue to grow in the ways I help Rob succeed with his life mission.

God has given *you* the unique job of helping *your* husband. My point here is not that my experiences in this area are universal to all marriages. I can just hear women saying, "Well, how can I help my husband with his business?" or, "How can I help him with his plumbing?" The answer is, "I don't know." I do not know how you are going to help your husband. The best way to start is to ask him. If you want to begin fulfilling your God-given job description, ask your husband how you can help him suc-

God has given *you* the unique job of helping *your* husband.

ceed today. Pray that God will guide and direct you as to how you can best help your husband, and for Him to give you the grace to embrace your role as a helper fit for him.

It is important to remember this is *God's* calling on your marriage and not your husband's idea. Adam did not give Eve her job description, God did. As we learn to be helpers to our husbands it is easy to expect something in return. If our attitude is based on helping our husbands so they will help us, we will not be rewarded. However, if we pray with sincere hearts for the Lord to turn our hearts towards our husbands, and we humbly embrace our role as a helper in our marriage, we will be blessed. The Lord will bless you even if your husband is not following his job description. There are always blessings for obedience.

Are you willing to embrace the first part of your purpose as a Christian wife? Are you willing to help? If you are, then you are taking a step closer to a visionary marriage.

Prayer (for wives):

Dear God,

I am bombarded with messages from the world about my role as a wife and my purpose as a woman. It is easy for me to listen to our culture, and even my own heart, more than I listen to Your Word. Help me to turn my heart to my husband. Remind me daily to think about how I can help him be successful. Give me the courage to ask him how I can best help him. I want to be the wife You created me to be.

In Jesus' name, Amen.

Prayer (for husbands):

Dear God,

You were right when You said it is not good for man to be alone. Show me when I am prideful, and when I believe I don't need help. Thank You for giving me my wife. I want to be the kind of man she wants to help. Let me love her, serve her, and lead her with a humble heart. Give me a compelling Christ-centered vision for our family.

In Jesus' name, Amen.

Questions for further thought and discussion

1. How do you first respond when you hear this God-given job description for a wife to be a helper fit for her husband?

2. How has modern culture impacted your thinking about the role of the Christian wife? How has it impacted the Christian church?

3. What obstacles do you face in fulfilling the mission of helping your husband be successful?

Reverence

In a biblical marriage, a wife is a helper fit for her husband. This is the first part of the job description that God gives us, and now we need to expand it further. The next passage we will look at is "the dreaded" Ephesians 5:22-33. This passage contains those two loaded words that have been, in recent years, hotly debated. Of course, I am referring to the 'S' word and the 'R' word. Dare I say it…"submit" and "respect." I can only imagine the enthusiasm you must be feeling!

Every Christian marriage book talks about Ephesians chapter 5. I am not going to say anything that others have not said before. However, biblical marriage has been assaulted in our culture and therefore we have to return once again to the basic building blocks for husbands and wives. My hope is that as you read this chapter, you will have a clearer understanding of your mission as a Christian wife. I hope you will desire to have your marriage sewn by the pattern of Scripture and not by the pattern of the world. I hope you will not strive to be a perfect wife, but a biblical wife.

As we jump right into this text, I want to remind you that I am not writing the message but simply delivering it. The Ephesians 5 text has been used in wedding ceremonies throughout church history because it directly addresses how a husband and wife should relate to one another. Because Rob has already demonstrated how a husband ought to love his wife, I will use this chapter to specifically focus on the directions given to wives.

Wives, submit to your own husbands, as to the Lord. For the husband is the head of the wife even as Christ is the head of the church, his body, and is himself its Savior. Now as the church submits to Christ, so also wives should submit in everything to their husbands.

EPHESIANS 5:22-24 ESV

However, let each one of you love his wife as himself, and let the wife see that she respects her husband.

EPHESIANS 5:33 ESV

My Way or God's Way

The Bible tells us, "Wives, submit to our own husbands, as to the Lord. For the husband is the head of the wife even as Christ is the head of the church..." If we are to submit to our husbands just as we submit to the Lord, then it might be helpful to first consider how we submit to the Lord.

According to the 1828 Webster Dictionary, the definition of "submit" is, "To yield, resign or surrender to the power, will or authority of another."[11] Submitting to the Lord means that we are choosing to live under God's authority. We willingly desire our will to be molded into God's will. We yield our right to have our own way. In reality, we all live under God's authority, some of us willingly and others unwillingly. The Bible is clear that someday every knee will bow...and every tongue will confess that Jesus is Lord (Philippians 2:10-11). As Christians, we choose to submit to God's authority today.

Sometimes Christians confuse avoiding sin with submission. Submission is not simply following a list of do's and don'ts. True submission to the Lord is evidenced when we are willing to go where He wants us to go and do what He wants us to do. You don't learn what it means to submit from a like-minded master. It would be easy to submit to the Lord if everything He asked us to do was exactly what we wanted to do. But we know that even Jesus, the second person of the Trinity, was asked to do what He never wanted to do. Jesus did not desire to die on a cross, but He surrendered His will to the will of God. He accepted God the Father's authority over His life.

In reality, we all live under God's authority, some of us willingly and others unwillingly.

So how does this relate to submitting to our husbands? First of all, we need to reject the idea that submission is a bad word. Unfortunately, even parts of the church have been infected with the world's attitude of entitlement when it comes to the issue of submission. If Jesus submitted to the will of His Father, why do we feel that it is unjust in this modern era to be called to submit to our husbands? Our first choice when we come to the Ephesians 5 passage is to ask ourselves if we are willing to submit our view of marriage to God's view of marriage. Will we yield to God's authority in our marriages? This is where submission begins.

"Wives, submit to your own husbands, *as to the Lord* (italics mine)" (Ephesians 5:22). If I am willing to submit myself to the authority of God's Word in my life and marriage, I can then pray for God to help me learn what it means to submit to my husband. Let us take a closer look at what that may look like in our marriages.

Authority and Accountability

Have you ever considered that our society is composed of institutions? There are the institutions of government, education, and business. As I mentioned in the previous chapter, God created the primary institution of society when He created families. Our society is not really made up of individuals, but of families. We have a plaque in our home that says, "Other things may change us, but we start and end with family."

In every institution of society there is always a leader. There is always a president, a CEO, a principal, or a chairperson of the board. The leader of any organization represents two things to the people of that organization. The leader has the ultimate authority and the ultimate accountability.

Ephesians 5:23 says, "For the husband is the head of the wife even as Christ is the head of the church..." When God created the family, the primary institution of society, He established the husband as the leader of that institution. Your husband has the ultimate authority over your marriage and the ultimate accountability for your marriage.

I must admit that I have always struggled with submitting to my husband's authority. There are two professions that I am convinced I could have excelled in if given the opportunity: lawyer and talk show host. I never shy away from an argument and I try to convince people that I am right. (We now have a daughter who is blessed with this ability.) My poor husband would often be forced to give in to my opinion out of sheer weariness. So at the beginning of my marriage, I did not think that I really had to submit to my husband because we were supposed to mutually submit to each other. But then, even after the Holy Spirit convicted me that I needed to learn to submit to Rob, I would argue him to death until he would agree with me...and then I would submit! If you are waiting for your husband to think like you before you start practicing submission, you will be waiting for a long time.

When I finally figured out that submitting to Rob meant doing it his way even if I disagreed with him, I began to see more blessings in our marriage. First of all, my respect for Rob dramatically increased. My heart for Rob changed, too. When I realized that he was accountable for our marriage in a way that I would never experience, I began to empathize with the load he carried. I might have wanted the authority, but I never wanted the greater accountability. Have you ever been persistent about doing things your way and then blaming your husband if the outcome was not what you expected? Of course, none us would do anything as ridiculous as that. So the next time you bite your lip and choose to submit when you disagree, please think of this simple truth. You are responsible to your husband, but your husband is responsible to you and for you. In other words, your husband carries a greater weight for your marriage than you do. You will never carry the weight of your marriage that God placed on your husband's shoulders.

> **Have you ever been persistent about doing things your way and then blaming your husband if the outcome was not what you expected?**

As I am writing this I am afraid you may be getting a picture of my home that would be quite opposite from reality. There are *many* times that Rob does things my way. There are *many* subjects in our home where Rob submits to my opinions and my expertise. *Most* of the time (well, pretty much all the time), Rob asks me where I want to go for dinner instead of choosing the restaurant himself. My willingness to submit has not led to "Rob-domination." Rather, it has led to my husband's growing love and confidence in leading our family. Isn't that what we all want for our husbands?

However, you must expect your husband to make mistakes, even big mistakes. Sometimes you will have to pray that God will help you keep your mouth closed and other times you will have to ask God how to talk to your husband about an important area of disagreement or concern. Your imperfect husband will make a lot of mistakes in leading your family just as you make mistakes every day. (A mark of our spiritual maturity is our awareness of the ongoing sin in our lives and our daily need for repentance and grace.) But even as he makes mistakes, remember your job description as a wife is to submit. In my marriage, this does not mean that I keep my opinions silent from my husband. It means that when Rob and I disagree, I am willing to submit to him.

Unfortunately, there are evil husbands. Some of you are in marriages where your husband does not have good intentions for you. As a therapist and a pastor's wife, I am not naïve about the harsh realities of some marriages. If this is the situation you are in, please understand that you should *never* submit to a man who abuses you or your children.[12] You should not submit to a man who encourages you to sin. I know that if you are in a difficult situation it has been torture to get through this section on submission. It is very painful to look at God's perfect blueprint for marriage when your own home is falling apart.

Respect and Reverence

At the end of Ephesians 5, Paul gives a concluding statement about the relationship between husbands and wives.

> *"However, let each one of you love his wife as himself, and let the wife see that she respects her husband."*

Ephesians 5:33 ESV

Husbands are called to love their wives and wives are called to respect their husbands. Why are wives called to *respect* as opposed to *love* their husbands? You may have had the opportunity to read the book *Love and Respect.*[13] This is an excellent marriage resource which goes into detail about the vital differences between men and women. It is especially helpful in giving practical applications for women to grow in an attitude of respect for their husbands. Rob and I benefited a great deal by attending a Love and Respect Conference.

However, Rob and I disagree with Eggrichs on a minor point. When dealing with the issue of why women are called to respect rather than love their husbands, he concludes that women do not need to be called to "love" because it is part of a woman's nature. His point is valid that women are generally more nurturing and affectionate than men. But when it comes to love, none of us do it naturally. I struggle respecting *and* loving my husband. Love does not come naturally for me; does it for you? As the mother of three girls and three boys, I do not find either sex having any advantage when it comes to learning to love. It is by the grace of God that we can love others.

So why are husbands called to love while wives are called to respect? I think our answer is found in the Ephesians text. As Rob talked about earlier in chapter 3, there are three Greek words for love: *eros*, *phileo*, and *agape*. In this text, the word used is *agape*. This word is often used to describe God's love for us. We find *agape* in what is perhaps the most famous verse in the Bible.

> *For God so loved (agape) the world, that he gave his only Son, that whoever believes in him should not perish but have eternal life.*

JOHN 3:16 ESV

It is *agape* love that is described in 1 Corinthians 13. It is God's model of love. *Agape* love is what we as Christians are praying for in our lives. We pray for the grace to love others, friends and enemies alike, with *agape* love. So in this manner, wives are called to love their husbands in the same sense we are called to love everyone.

However, there is no *specific* commandment in Scripture for wives to *agape* love their husbands, while there is this specific commandment for husbands to *agape* love their wives. If we look again at Ephesians (you must have it all memorized by now), the explanation of this difference is inherent in the text. "Husbands must love their wives *as Christ loved the church and gave himself up for her*" (italics mine). Whose love is stronger? Christ's love for the church or the church's love for Christ? Christ's love for the church is more powerful than the church's love for Christ. Jesus Christ willingly sacrificed His life for the church. While the church may be asked to suffer and die for Christ, none of this would have been possible without His sacrificial death. As the Scripture says, "We love Him because he first loved us" (1 John 4:19, ESV). A husband is commanded to love his wife with a greater love than God specifically requires from his wife.

The Meaning of a Word

One of the things we have been working on in our home is carefully choosing our words. The best example of this is the word "love." In the Rienow family, we do not use the word love in connection with anything other than God and people (and pets to a lesser degree). For example, we do not say, "I love ice cream" or, "I love this game," because it is clear in Scripture that God wants us to love people, not things. So we say, "I really like ice cream" or "I am fond of this game" (the kids don't really say that, but you get the point). My six-year-old Laynie does an excellent job of reminding all of us of the "love" rule, including Mom, whose tongue can slip into old habits.

Wives are called to respect their husbands. I have enjoyed studying that word more closely. The Greek word that is translated as "respect," in translations such as the ESV and NIV, is *phobetai*, which literally means, "to fear." This word is used in Scripture in a variety of ways. We are probably most familiar with the concept of "fearing the Lord." This means having a holy awe of God and His Word. Here in Ephesians, as it relates to husbands and wives, the word is most commonly translated as "respect" or in the case of the King James Version as "reverence." The most comprehensive Greek-English lexicon of the New Testament and early Christian literature affirms these two possible translations of "reverence" and "respect."[14]

Now this is where it gets interesting. I looked up respect and reverence in my 1828 Noah Webster Dictionary. I highly recommend getting this particular edition in your home because it is filled with Christian theology and themes. Webster frequently refers to Scripture, and uses Scripture as a part of his definitions for words. Here are the definitions of respect and reverence:

Respect: To view or consider with some degree of reverence; to esteem as possessed of real worth.

Reverence: To regard with fear (awe) mingled with respect and affection. Reverence is nearly equivalent to veneration but expresses something less of the same emotion.

After studying these words I was curious about veneration.

Veneration: The highest degree of respect and reverence.

Here is how this simple word study has helped me to better understand and apply God's commandment to wives in Ephesians. The three words, respect, reverence and veneration increase in intensity. Respect is the most common word. I want to treat all people with respect. I think veneration is best used to describe my attitude towards God. Yet, I want to have a special and unique respect for my husband. Therefore, it has been helpful for me to use the word reverence when I reflect on how I want to treat Rob. I desire to treat Rob with greater respect than I treat others. When my goal is to reverence my husband, I feel I am giving him special attention that is reserved for him alone. I hope this distinction is helpful for you.

Before we look at practical ways we can reverence our husbands, I hope you have come to appreciate the difference between these two callings on husbands and wives. To respect or reverence is not a more difficult calling than to love. In fact, in some ways the command given to wives may be less difficult. Would you like to trade commands with your husband? I would answer, "No." It is humbling to consider that our husbands are called to lay down their lives for us. Now, I am not saying your husband is succeeding at following God's command of sacrificial love, but he will

It is humbling to consider that our husbands are called to lay down their lives for us. answer to God for his actions. We also will stand before God one day and answer for our actions. Let us strive to fulfill the command to respect and reverence our husbands that God has given us.

How does a Wife Reverence her Husband?

I will never forget the day I was exposed to some amazing teaching about the power of a wife's reverence towards her husband. I had decided to take a bath to unwind after a long day. As I was relaxing, I was listening to a sermon by S.M. Davis (one of my favorite preachers) entitled, "How a Wife can use Reverence to Honor her Husband." At this point in my marriage, I was already convicted of the importance of respecting Rob. In fact, by God's grace, I was making progress in this area. Yet, as I sat in the bath, the weight of the conviction of the Holy Spirit became so heavy that I was no longer unwinding, but weeping. I repented and asked God to give me a new vision for fulfilling this role God had given me.

One of the best ways I can show reverence to Rob is by freely praising him. When we were first married, I am ashamed to say that I tended to be critical of him. When he would preach to the youth group, he would often feel charged and energized after his sermon was over. He would receive several compliments from students and adults. While I was very proud of him and always thought that he did a great job, I felt that I had to offer tips to "fine tune" his preaching. During the car ride home, he was often greeted with a token "great job" and then a list of my critiques. Sadly, I could see the energy deflate out of him like a balloon. This was not what I was intending, but this was the result of my critical remarks. Unfortunately, this happened on one too many occasions. Rob gently told me that my praises meant more to him than all the accolades of others. He told me that if he had my praises, he could handle the criticism of others. But if he did not sense my approval, than the praises of others were rather empty. Part of Rob's God-given mission in the world is his work at church, and he needs my support.

Your husband needs to know that you admire him. It is good to praise him both privately and publicly. When we praise our husbands publicly we magnify the power of our words. A humble man will not sing his own praises, nor should he. As I remind my children, "Let another praise you, and not your own mouth" (Proverbs 27:2). But men love to be praised by their wives in front of other men. God has designed your husband's heart to respond to your reverence. The more you praise him, the less likely he will be to seek affirmation elsewhere.

Conversely, if we criticize our husbands publicly (whether he is around to hear it or not) we are dealing our husbands a severe blow. I am reminded of a time when I was at a meeting at church with a mixed group of people including an older married couple. During the meeting, the husband asked a question that may have seemed obvious to others but apparently was not to him. Before the leader could respond to the question, his wife answered him in a way that clearly expressed her belief in the absurdity of his question. I instantly sunk back in my chair as I watched the look of embarrassment and shame come across his face. It is one thing to say something that may be embarrassing in front of a group, but it is quite another to have your wife be the one who mocks you.

God has designed your husband's heart to respond to your reverence. The more you praise him, the less likely he will be to seek affirmation elsewhere.

Another way I seek to show reverence to Rob is by expressing gratitude for him and the things he does. Many Generation X women like myself may find themselves struggling here. We were raised in a culture which taught us that men and women can and *should* do all the same things. When both spouses are contributing to the family finances and tackling daily household chores, wives may be less likely to say "Thank you." If you do not expect to be thanked when you do the dishes, why should you thank your husband when he does them? In fact, we expect him to carry his fair share of the work. Yet our husbands need to know that we appreciate them. By thanking your husband frequently you are showing reverence to him.

Finally, one of the most meaningful ways I seek to reverence Rob is by forgiving him easily. Forgiveness is hard in marriage. Why can it be easier to forgive a co-worker than it is to forgive your own husband? First of all, in a marriage you have to learn to forgive the same offenses time and time again. Secondly, your husband has the most potential to hurt you because he is the closest to you. I had a horrible habit in my marriage that I still fight against now. When I felt really hurt by Rob I would "put him in the doghouse" (those are Rob's words and not mine). This meant that instead of forgiving the hurt quickly, I would punish him by withdrawing from the relationship for a time period. I rationalized that I needed my space, but really, I was slow to forgive. This hurt him. I praise God for His grace which has enabled me to repent of my attitude as I now seek to practice forgiving him quickly.

These are just some of the ways that I am trying to reverence my husband and therefore to obey the Ephesians 5:33 command. I encourage you to pray and ask God to give you a specific plan for how you can show more reverence and respect to your husband.

Prayer (for wives):

Dear God,

Thank You for my husband. Help me to believe Your Word and accept the mission You have given me to submit and reverence my husband. Even saying those words is difficult. I need You to change my heart and give me Your grace. Lead me to specific and practical ways that I can show him respect, even when I feel he doesn't deserve it. Help me to submit to my husband, as to You.

In Jesus' name, Amen.

Prayer (for husbands):

Dear God,

Thank You for my wife. I am humbled to know You call my wife to respect me. I know You call her to respect me even when I don't deserve it, but I want to do everything I can to earn her respect. Please make it easier and easier for her to respect me in the days and years ahead. The only way this will happen is if You make me more like Christ. I want You to make me more pure, more responsible, and more loving. Thank You that You promise to complete me in Christ.

In Jesus' name, Amen.

Questions for further thought and discussion

1. For wives—What has your experience been in talking about the issues of submission and respect with other Christian women?

2. In your church, is there more specific teaching about what the Bible says to men or to women? If there is a difference, why do you think that is?

3. For wives—how can you express concerns about your marriage and family to your husband in a respectful way?

CHAPTER 9

Training

Now that we have studied two famous texts in Scripture that are written to women, we are going to shift our attention to a text that may not be as familiar. We won't cover every passage written to women, but I encourage you to take that journey on your own. Titus 2:3-5 will be the third major text we examine about God's mission for the Christian wife.

There are two reasons I think this passage is helpful for us to study. First, it is a New Testament passage that gives specific directions to women in the church. The book of Titus gives us a list of character qualities for God's people. In Titus there are specific instructions for older and younger women. Many women's mentoring ministries are based on Titus 2.

The second reason that I chose Titus 2 is based on my own experience in the church. Even though I grew up in a Bible church, actively involved in my youth group, I had no direct teaching on this passage of Scripture. When I was participating in college ministries, I do not recall spending time studying Titus. And during my time at a Christian graduate school, I never studied this Scripture and how it related to marriage. This is interesting because I was studying to be a Christian marriage and family therapist! Titus 2 is certainly relevant for developing biblical marriages. Even in my women's Bible studies at church, I don't remember Titus 2 being emphasized.

Maybe I just blanked out or was absent every time Titus was taught in my study groups. I am not trying to point blame at the spiritual leaders that instructed me. Nevertheless, I was already married with three children before I began reading books based on these verses. I felt that I would have been better served had I spent more time thinking about the directions in Titus 2:3-5 *before* I got married and started raising a family.

Older women likewise are to be reverent in behavior, not slanderers or slaves to much wine. They are to teach what is good, and so train the young women to love their husbands and children, to be self-controlled, pure, working at home, kind, and submissive to their own husbands, that the word of God may not be reviled.

TITUS 2:3-5 ESV

As you can see, these verses are apt to raise controversy. This is probably why I did not study this text as a girl, a college student, or a young woman. However, even if we ignore God's Word, it is not going away. The question we have to personally deal with is "Do I believe this is the truth?" If we do not believe the Bible is true, then we can ignore what it says. Yet, if we profess the Bible is God's truth, then we have to deal with what it says even if His Word makes us uncomfortable.

Trained to Love

Older women are to teach the younger women "what is good." The beginning of this teaching is to "train the young women to love their husbands and children."

When I think of the word "to train," two things come to my mind: a marathon runner and my ill-behaved dogs. Training implies a lot of hard work. When we were first married, I had a lot of work to do in any given day. There was work from my job, housework and ministry at church. Loving Rob was supposed to be the easy part of my day, not hard work. This misguided expectation caused a lot of unhappiness in our marriage. If I was not having "loving" feelings towards Rob, I began to doubt our relationship. It is easier to blame a relationship than to blame yourself. While I had often heard that marriage was hard work, I did not realize that I needed to commit time and energy to the task of loving my husband. Yet, in Titus this is what older women are to be training younger women to do.

Yet, if we profess the Bible is God's truth, then we have to deal with what it says even if His Word makes us uncomfortable.

I often expected loving Rob to come naturally. Yet naturally, none of us are very good lovers. If you find it difficult to love your husband, do not be discouraged. Do not believe the lie that there is something wrong with your marriage. Loving your husband requires training. It requires hard work. When you consider the work you have to do in a given day, do you think about how you can love your husband even better than the day before?

Are you fond of your man?

This may sound confusing in light of the last chapter. Do you remember that wives are not given the specific command in Scripture to *agape* love their husbands? That is what is interesting about this direction to women in Titus. The Greek word used for love in this verse is *phileo*. The word literally means, "to be fond of." This is brotherly love, or companion love. For example, Philadelphia, the city of brotherly love, comes from this Greek word. This type of love is different than agape love. Here in Titus, wives are instructed to *phileo* love their husbands. What does that mean?

It makes me sad to think about this but I remember in the early years of our marriage Rob would sometimes say to me, "I know that you love me, but sometimes I feel that you don't like me." Unfortunately, Rob was reading my feelings well. I loved Rob and I was committed to him, but I was not "*phileo* loving" him. I was not meeting his need to be liked. His feelings were largely due to my negative attitude about little things. I may not have liked the way he had dressed, or I was annoyed that he did not have the social manners that I expected. Most of the things that bothered me were very minor, but these pet peeves eroded my *phileo* love for Rob. It was no wonder Rob did not feel that I liked him.

A small part of every man is an insecure boy. The book *Rocking the Roles* by Robert Lewis, does an excellent job of explaining this issue.[15] Our husbands need to feel our approval of who they are. This is exactly the direction given to wives in the book of Titus. Older women need to train younger women to *phileo* love their husbands. Literally, it could be translated to "be fond of" their husbands. When you are fond of your husband, you are giving him the companion love that he needs. It requires training to love your husband in this way. You need to be aware of his personal insecurities so you can be the one who affirms him in the areas he needs the most.

If a woman has a son, it is easier for her to understand this. I know how much my boys desire my approval. They love to demonstrate their abilities for me. When I praise them, I bolster feelings of security. If I am critical, they can feel torn down and defeated. Our husbands need this kind of love from us. If they feel our approval, they will feel more secure in their work outside the home. When they show off their abilities, praise them. Compliment your husband for all the godly character traits your see in him. This is even more important when he is experiencing difficulties at work. If your husband is dealing with rejection at work, make sure he receives your acceptance at home. Train yourself to love your husband by liking him!

> **You need to be aware of his personal insecurities so that you can be the one who affirms him in the areas he needs the most.**

Self-Controlled and Pure

In Titus 2:5, young women are directed to be "self-controlled and pure." These seem overly general. Everyone should strive to be self-controlled and pure. Yet according to this verse, these are character traits that young women

If your husband is dealing with rejection at work, make sure he receives your acceptance at home.

especially ought to possess. If the Scripture says it, then I want to apply it to my life. Being self-controlled and pure must be essential for a Christian wife.

Sometimes, I believe women in our current evangelical Christian culture are given a spiritual pass. I have heard many sermons preached from the pulpit admonishing men for specific sins. The biggest example is pornography. It is common for pastors to call out men to live lives of integrity. I have even heard Father's Day sermons that admonish men to be sexually pure. This is not a warm, fuzzy, encouraging sermon for men, but a bold confrontation about an area of sin that most men either struggle with or have struggled with in their lives.

Have you ever heard a Mother's Day sermon that admonishes women for dressing immodestly? I have not. This is what I mean by a "spiritual pass." There is a politically correct culture in the evangelical church of America that often inhibits pastors from directly confronting women about areas of sin that most women struggle with in their lives. Modesty is one of these topics. With the way many women dress today, men do not have to look far to find pornography! How is a man supposed to be sexually pure when the woman sitting in the pew next to him is wearing a low-cut, see-through shirt? In my experience, specific admonitions to men abound without corresponding challenges to women.

As Christian wives, we should strive to be self-controlled and pure. These two character traits are important for dealing with areas of sin that women struggle with in our culture. A good example of this is gossip. In my experience, women struggle with gossip more than men. I know I have had to deal with this sin in my life. Remember I mentioned my talk show host skills? I am an extrovert who does not shy away from conversation or sharing my opinions. Conversation is good. Gossip is evil. Being married to a pastor caused me to pay more attention to this sin in my life. Because of my husband's position in the church, I had to choose carefully the words coming out of my mouth. The power of the tongue cannot be overstated. Read this warning in James 3.

So also the tongue is a small member, yet it boasts of great things. How great a forest is set ablaze by such a small fire! And the tongue is a fire, a world of unrighteousness. The tongue is set among our members, staining the whole body, setting on fire the entire course of life, and set on fire by hell. For every kind of beast and bird, of reptile and sea creature, can be tamed and has been tamed by mankind, but no human being can tame the tongue. It is a restless evil, full of deadly poison. With it we bless our Lord and Father, and with it we curse people who are made in the likeness of God.

JAMES 3:5-9 ESV

Christian wives are called to be self-controlled and our words are an important place to start. I am not just talking about the words we say out of the home, but inside the home as well. If we are bad-mouthing family members (this does include your mother-in-law) to our children, we are spreading evil in our own homes. Our words should bring blessings to our family, not curses. I realize there is a fine line between sharing your troubles with a friend for prayer and support versus gossip. Gossip is sharing something negative about a person with the intent of hurting that person, or desiring the hearer to think less of that individual. Christian women need to take this sin seriously. We will not be perfect in this area but this should remind us not to expect perfection from our husbands in their areas of weakness either. When we do gossip, we should repent and apologize to those we have offended. God desires us to be self-controlled with our tongues.

God also directs young women to be pure. One of the jobs I had as a therapist was facilitating a support group for women whose husbands were dealing with sexual addictions. I remember when a Victoria's Secret fashion show was going to be aired on prime-time television. The women were outraged. I wish more Christian women would share that outrage. Not just wives, but Christian women are called to be pure. I praise God for His grace alone that convicted me about shopping at Victoria's Secret early in my marriage. This one store alone greatly increased soft pornography in our culture. In fact, our husbands, sons, and brothers do not have a choice about viewing this type of pornography because they are surrounded by it. Yet, if more women were dedicated to purity as opposed to sexiness, there would not be the market for stores such as these. Christian wives, biblical wives, need to take seriously this direction

When we do gossip, we should repent and apologize to those we have offended.

to be pure for the sake of their husbands, sons, and daughters. Be wise about where you shop, and the magazines you allow in your home. Your purity directly influences your husband's purity.

Working at Home

Now we get to the direction to young wives in Titus that is likely to cause the most controversy. To be honest, I think this one phrase "working at home" is the primary reason I was not familiar with this text even though I was raised in a Bible-teaching church. Unfortunately, even in churches that preach the Bible, we may not be taught the *whole* Bible. But I cannot blame my church, because the culpability falls on me alone. I have been a Christian since I was four-years-old, but I had not read the entire Bible (every single book) until I was in my twenties. I consider that disgraceful. If I sincerely believed the Bible to be God's truth, then why had I not read it at least 10 times through by the time

I hit twenty! I do not want to give you the wrong impression. People would have considered me to be very Bible-literate. I had memorized Bible verses since the time I was little, and I read my daily Bible devotions from the beginning of high school. But I did not read the Bible from cover to cover like I would naturally read other books. It is important that we read the Bible in its entirety if we want to be students of God's truth.

The phrase "working at home" comes from the Greek word, *oikourous*. This word literally means "working at home, staying at home, domestic."[16] This is the way this word is represented in various English translations

- working at home (English Standard Version)
- busy at home (New International Version)
- having care of the house (Wycliffe's New Testament)
- workers at home (American Standard Version)
- homemakers (New King James Version)
- keepers at home (King James Version)

Regardless of the translation, this phrase emphasizes the wife's role of working in, caring for, and keeping the home. This is a special direction given to wives, not to husbands.

Voddie Baucham, in his book, *Family Driven Faith* refers to the wife as the COO of the home.[17] She is the Chief Operating Officer while the husband functions as the Chief Executive Officer. The home runs best when the husband and the wife are working together in their respective positions. The Christian wife understands that she is the keeper of the home. A COO sounds like a fairly important position, doesn't it? It is not a job we should take lightly.

Now when many of us hear the phrase "Chief Operating Officer" our stress level begins to elevate. Does this mean I am obligated to do all the cooking, cleaning, ironing, grocery shopping and take care of all the children's needs by myself? Being the keeper of the home does not mean you have to do all the jobs in the home alone. The COO *manages* the responsibilities of the home. Running a family requires a lot of work. In a healthy family, there is a balanced division of labor between husband, wife and children.

Unfortunately, I did not embrace this COO position in the early years of our marriage because I believed I *needed* to be successful in a career. Spending so much time, money, and energy on academic pursuits, it seemed ridiculous to not use my degrees to find work outside the home. When Rob and I were both working in ministry I also worked as a therapist. Managing the home did not take that much time and it did not seem to matter very much. The home was simply the staging ground for the next *important* activity.

When Rob and I began having children, I became much more aware of the environment of our home. As two fast-paced people, we often had

> **In a healthy family, there is a balanced division of labor between husband, wife and children.**

chaotic days. In most homes with small children there are chaotic days. It is okay to have difficult days and weeks, but I did not want the normal atmosphere of our home to feel hectic and hurried for my husband and children. In order to have peace in the home, I needed to be a better *keeper* of the home. A wife's character has a dramatic affect on the entire home. Have you ever seen this bumper sticker? "If Mama ain't happy, ain't nobody happy." While that may be an overstatement, the truth is that our actions and attitudes shape and influence every aspect of family life. As a Christian wife, God has assigned you as the *keeper* of the home.

Isn't that the main point of Proverbs 31? Proverbs 31 is about a godly wife who manages her home well. While I frequently studied that passage before I was married, I did not apply it as literally as I should have. Most of the studies I did were focused on the general character traits that compose a godly woman. This proverb is helpful for all Christian women. Yet, when a girl becomes a wife, Proverbs 31 is a biblical guideline for helping a woman to learn home management skills. It is a lofty description of a wonderful wife, but it is difficult to embrace if we feel we are hopelessly missing the mark. We are often harder on ourselves than God is. We are all called to live like Christ. While we obviously fall short of His example, we do not reject the calling. Do not reject the calling of a Proverbs 31 wife even if you feel you fall short of it. God will bless our efforts to live according to His Word.

Let's address the elephant in the room. If God requires us to be working in the home, does it mean we are not supposed to be working outside of the home? That was the consensus opinion in western culture for a considerable time. While it is outdated, we are all familiar with the phrase, "a woman's place is in the home." As we can see from this passage in Titus, this type of thinking does have its roots in Scripture. American culture, in particular, was largely built by Christian families who lived according to these principles. Throughout the twentieth century, particularly in the 1960s, the influential feminist movement altered this view of the home. It was not that women in the past had not worked outside of the home because they did. But now the expectation was that women *should* have careers outside of their homes. Being a part of Generation X, I was taught to think this way. When I was in school, I never thought it would be alright to "just" be a wife and a mother. I believed I should pursue not just a job, but a career.

There is no commandment in the Bible that forbids a woman from working outside of her home. In fact, the Proverbs 31 wife works in the community as a part of the family business. It really is a matter of priorities. The question we have to ask ourselves is, "Which work is the priority of our hearts?" There is nothing wrong with working outside of the home, as long as we are able to be good keepers of our home. God's priorities for our marriages need to be our first priorities. We also need to submit to our husband's leadership when it comes to decisions about work outside our homes.

> **When I was in school, I never thought it would be alright to "just" be a wife and a mother.**

When we were newly married, the vision I had for the purpose of our home was very small. Truthfully, I had no spiritual vision for my home at all. I primarily thought of my home in terms of how it was decorated. On a pastor's income, my home was never decorated the way I imagined it could be, but I did the best I could. I spent time painting old furniture and designing curtains with my mom because I had a vision about how I wanted the home to look. I desired to have a beautiful home like every young bride. However, if a beautiful home is the extent of your vision, a good trip to IKEA may be all you need.

By the grace of God, I now have a much greater vision for my work at home. I view my home as the place where Rob and I are training our children to be godly men and women, and hopefully future husbands and wives. I realize that our home is the primary place where we will all grow as a family in godly character. I want to create an environment where my husband longs to come back to when he is finished at work. I want my home to be a place of spiritual refreshment. I desire peace in my home. May it be a place where we learn to deal with conflict biblically and forgiveness flows easily. As Christians, we are the light of the world. I long for our home to reflect that light through hospitality, and that spirit of hospitality begins with the way I serve my own husband and children. While I used to be concerned about so many things outside of my home, I am now far more concerned with what happens between our own four walls. I know that if we cannot learn to serve each other at home, then any service we are doing outside of the home will not be authentic. Sometimes the weight of what Rob and I are trying to accomplish in our family seems far too great. Yet I am so excited about the vision God has given me for my work at home. My home is still far from decorated the way I would like it to be, but I am truly thankful for the spiritual beauty I see taking place every day, in good times and bad.

I know this is an emotionally challenging topic for most women. Some of us are thriving in our careers and don't really want to think about making home a priority. Others are longing to be home but circumstances prevent us from being there. And some of us just feel that we are not doing a good job as keepers of our home. Many of us feel like we are failing on all fronts. Please do not be discouraged, whatever your situation may be. God's grace is abundant for us all. He meets us *all* right where we are. I hope a biblical vision of your role in the home will guide you in your future decisions.

Kind

Finally, Christian wives are instructed to be kind. Wives are to be, "self-controlled, pure, working at home, kind, and submissive to their own husbands, that the Word of God may not be reviled." While we have already discussed the issue of submission, it would be helpful to consider the importance of kindness in our marriages.

While most people that I am acquainted with would consider me to be a kind person, I am humbled by the admonition to be kind in this verse. Kindness is essential in winning anyone's heart. While I realize this, it is a spiritual battle to be consistently kind in my own home. Have you ever had the experience of your children speaking to each other in an ugly way only to realize they learned it from you? Unfortunately, I have. Sometimes I can't stand the sound of my own harsh reprimands. Whether we are yelling in anger or speaking in a sarcastic, biting tone, these types of words will have the effect of closing our husbands' and children's hearts. A biblically grounded wife actively seeks to elevate kindness in her home.

Have you ever had the experience of your children speaking to each other in an ugly way only to realize they learned it from you?

Just the other night I was speaking with a friend who has been dealing with a teenage daughter's rebellious attitude. As she was expressing her hurt and frustration, she reminded me of the need for kindness.

She said that the Lord had encouraged her in her quiet time that morning through the verse:

> *Or do you presume on the riches of his kindness and forbearance and patience, not knowing that God's kindness is meant to lead you to repentance?*
>
> ROMANS 2:4 ESV

What an excellent motivation for us to strive to speak kind words to our husbands and our children!

May the Word of God not be reviled

Indeed, this is a strong conclusion to our text. These directions given to wives are followed with this warning, "that the Word of God may not be reviled." Living according to God's Word is difficult in our culture today. Most aspects of secular culture are in opposition to God's ways. Praise God that we do not live in a society where we are persecuted for following His commands. Therefore, in our free society, we may have an even greater responsibility to live in light of the Word God has entrusted to His people. My prayer is that Christian wives will embrace their mission from God in a way that transforms the culture in which we live. May the Word of God not be reviled in our generation!

Prayer (for wives):

Dear God,

Please expand my vision for my role and calling as a Christian wife. Help me to submit my way of thinking to Your way of thinking. Please train me to love my husband the way You call me to and help me to be a blessing to everyone in my home. Turn my heart toward the ministry of my home. I want to excel and succeed as the keeper of my home. Guard my heart from other loves and impurity. Give me the self-control that I don't have on my own. Give me the grace to live at home in such a way that Your Word would be honored.

In Jesus' name, Amen.

Prayer (for husbands):

Dear God,

Thank You for my wife. You brought us together to bring glory to Your Son Jesus. You have given my wife a big responsibility and calling as described in Titus 2. I want to encourage her to trust You in everything. Help me encourage faith in her heart. Please give me the grace to give my best care, love, and leadership to her. Thank You for expanding our vision for our marriage. Keep us moving forward, for Your glory.

In Jesus' name, Amen.

Questions for further thought and discussion

1. How would you define the difference between liking and loving your husband? Pray for God to help you succeed in both.

2. In your experience, do you see Christian churches shying away from challenging women in areas of gossip, purity, and modesty?

3. How has your view and understanding of a wife's role in the home been impacted by your education and the culture around you?

Two Shall
Become One

*For this reason a man will leave his father and mother and
be united to his wife, and they will become one flesh.*

GENESIS 2:24

When God first created the blessing and institution of marriage, He described a three-fold process. We are called to leave, unite our lives, and to become one. It is worth noting that the world encourages us to reverse the order. Unite sexually, build a relationship, and then move out of your parent's house! Perhaps you have heard this Scripture in the more traditional language of leaving, cleaving, and becoming one. Many marriage problems are directly traceable to a breakdown in one or more of these areas. If the husband is still calling his mother for advice every day, that is going to be a problem. He has not "left" well. If the wife is prioritizing relationships with old college roommates ahead of her husband, a marriage crisis is on the way. She has not "cleaved" or "united with" her husband.

While many marriage issues can be traced to dysfunction in the areas of "leaving" or "cleaving," our focus will be on the ultimate goal—two becoming one. True unity between husband and wife is a reflection of the character and nature of God. The more your hearts, souls, and lives are unified, the more your marriage honors God and points others toward Him.

When we got married, we had a fairly clear understanding of the first two parts. We needed to leave our parents' homes, and begin a new family with independent jurisdiction. It was also clear to us that we had to build our new life together. We had to find a house or apartment. We combined our finances. Amy got a new last name. Our lives "cleaved" together. Our time, focus, relationships, interests, and hobbies had to shift and change. We talk with many young couples who have bought the lie that married life is just like single life, except you are married. Nothing could be further from the truth. When you get married, you are exchanging an individual life for a together life. Everything changes. Friendships change. Personal relationships with people of the opposite sex dramatically diminish. Hobbies increasingly shift to the margin of your schedule. If a person doesn't want these things to happen, they shouldn't get married!

The Unity Candle

As we mentioned in an earlier chapter, we did not build our marriage with a solid biblical foundation. We did not allow Scripture to establish the vision for our marriage. Even in our wedding ceremony, we made a conscious choice to declare our independence rather than our new unity as husband and wife. After we made our vows to one another and exchanged rings, we used a unity candle to symbolize our

> **When you get married, you are exchanging an individual life for a together life.**

marriage. Perhaps you had a unity candle at your wedding. Just prior to the ceremony, our mothers had gone up on the platform and lit two candles representing each of us. In-between these two lit candles stood the larger and taller "unity" candle. We both took our individual candles and combined the flames to light the candle in the middle. Then, instead of blowing out our individual candles we left them lit, and returned them to their original places. We talked at length prior to the ceremony about this moment. We wanted to make it clear to ourselves, and to those present, that just because we were getting married we were not sacrificing or diminishing our individuality. The tradition of the unity candle is designed for a very simple purpose, to give visual representation of Genesis 2:24. The ceremony starts with two lights, two individuals, and it ends with one light representing the one marriage. The two become one. In our ceremony, however, the two lights became three!

Jesus taught frequently on the subject of marriage, and often pointed people back to God's original design for marriage and family as revealed by God in Genesis. But Jesus did more than quote the Genesis texts. He expanded upon them in an effort to drive home the truth of God's Word even further. Consider these words from Jesus.

> *But at the beginning of creation God 'made them male and female.' 'For this reason a man will leave his father and mother and be united to his wife, and the two will become one flesh.' So they are no longer two, but one.*
>
> MARK 10:6-8

Look at the last sentence. These words represent Jesus' expansion and emphasis regarding the Genesis 2 text. He affirms that God desires husband and wife to leave, cleave, and become one, and then to make sure that there would be no confusion He adds, "they are no longer two, but one."

Glorified Roommates

We were on track to becoming glorified roommates. Amy had her goals, ambitions, dreams, and priorities. Rob had his goals, ambitions, dreams, and priorities. We deeply cared about one another. We had sex. We organized our home. We had children and loved raising them. Amy was working part-time as a counselor and Rob was focused on ministry at church. We both volunteered but often in different areas. Home was the place we made our transition in-between the important things we were doing outside. It was true that we lived together and acted like a married couple, but the two had not become one. We did not have a shared, compelling, biblical purpose for our lives.

We were on track to becoming glorified roommates.

So what does it really look like for a husband and wife not just to leave and cleave, but to truly become one? What happens when a man lives out his mission to love, serve, and lead while at the same time a wife embraces her mission to help him succeed?

Two Keys

Have you ever seen one of those political thriller movies where two soldiers are deep in a secret bunker waiting for the orders to launch the missiles? Each one has his hand on a key. For the missiles to launch, both people must turn their keys.

Many husbands and wives are waiting for their spouse to make changes before they are willing to do anything different themselves. You turn your key first, and then I will turn mine! So the wife says, "As soon as I see you starting to love, serve, and lead, then I will start helping, respecting, and submitting." The man replies, "Well, as soon as I get some respect around here, then I will love you more. How can I love someone who treats me the way you do?" Then round and round we go. [18]

Struggling marriages are often locked in "blame mode." As the woman considers her marriage and family her thoughts go something like this, "If my husband would just show me more affection, be less harsh with the kids, realize that his work schedule is killing the family, and lead family devotions then everything around here would change." His thoughts move in the same direction, "If my wife would stop being so anxious about everything, have a positive attitude, stop treating me like a child, and quit being reckless with our money then everything around here would change." There are two reasons why "blame mode" is easy to get into and hard to leave. First, just as with our first parents Adam and Eve, our sinful nature always wants to blame others for the problems and suffering in our life. Second, the list of concerns you have about your spouse is probably totally legitimate. If your spouse *did* make these changes your family *would* change dramatically.

But here is the problem. When both of you are in blame mode, your marriage won't change. All your energy is focused on your spouse's problems and shortcomings. How is it working for you? Is your spouse changing? Probably not. Blame mode is not effective for bringing about change in your spouse. It is like one soldier, who is not turning his missile key, sitting there obsessing about why the other guy is not turning his!

So who should go first? Should the husband start loving, serving, and leading? Or should the wife start helping, respecting, and submitting? Eggerichs has a great answer to this. He suggests that "the more mature person" should go first. Ponder that for a moment, and you will quickly see his point.

> **When both of you are in blame mode, your marriage won't change. All your energy is focused on your spouse's problems and shortcomings.**

But my husband doesn't deserve my respect! My wife is so critical and negative, how could I ever love her? God addresses this for us back in the Ephesians 5 text. "Husbands, love your wives, *as Christ loved the church...*" Do we deserve the unconditional love of Christ? Have we earned His love with our exceptional behavior, character, and perfect holiness? Obviously, not! We don't deserve the love of Christ, yet He loves us. Ladies, here is a difficult question for you. Do you deserve the unconditional love of your husband? Have you earned his love with your exceptional behavior, character, and perfect holiness? Once again, the answer is no. It isn't meant to be harsh, but wives don't deserve the unconditional love of their husbands. Ladies, don't act like you deserve the unconditional love of your husband. You don't! Men, if you are waiting for perfection from your wife before you start showing her love, you are going to be waiting for a long time. Wives don't deserve the unconditional love of their husbands, and yet, what are husbands commanded to do? Love their wives, just as Christ loved the church. A husband is to give his wife what she doesn't deserve.

Let's consider the other side of the equation. Husbands, do you deserve the respect of your wife? Have you earned it with your exemplary character and holy behavior? The answer is the same, no! Men, don't demand respect, because you have not earned it, and remember that you don't *deserve* it. So husbands don't deserve the respect of their wives, and yet, what are wives commanded to do? Respect their husbands. A wife is to give her husband what he doesn't deserve.

Turn *Your* Key

In order to launch a visionary marriage, both husband and wife must embrace their God-given roles and responsibilities. They must both *turn their own key.* The best way to do this is for both husband and wife to submit themselves to God's Word and turn their keys at the same time. But in many marriages, one spouse makes the choice to submit to God's instructions before the partner does. They turn their key, and then pray and give themselves to helping their partner make the same choice. It is better to have one key turned than none. It is better for one person to embrace God's plan for the marriage and family, and be waiting for the other person to make the same choice than for both husband and wife to remain in rebellion against God and hard-hearted toward one another.

If someone has to be the first to turn their key, let it be you. Not only can your individual choice to please God set into motion a series of events which can transform your family, but whether your marriage changes or not, you are still accountable to God for the choices you make as a husband or wife.

Combining Job Descriptions

Throughout our journey through the key passages on marriage in the Bible, we have been focusing on the distinct roles that God has given to husbands and wives. Now we need to talk about how those roles come together into a single mission. Remember what Jesus said? *They are no longer two,* but one. God wants your job descriptions to combine together for a shared mission and purpose.

Perhaps the best way to illustrate the bringing together of these distinct roles is to consider the wife's calling to *help* her husband and *submit* to him. One of the greatest challenges for Christian women is that both of these words and roles are relative. They hinge on and are defined by her husband.

Imagine your best friend calls you on Friday afternoon. You answer the phone and are met with a question, "Hey, can you come over tomorrow and help me?" Your first response would probably be, "Sure." You would then quickly follow up with the question, "What are we doing?" The reason you need the follow-up question is that "Can you come over tomorrow and help me?" doesn't really mean anything. It doesn't provide any specifics. If your friend answered, "I need help taking care of the kids," then the request to *help* now means *take care of kids.* If your friend said, "I need help moving some wood," then *helping* means *moving wood.* *Help* is a relative term and needs further definition.

> **It is better for one person to embrace God's plan for the marriage and family, and be waiting for the other person to make the same choice than for both husband and wife to remain in rebellion against God and hard-hearted toward one another.**

The same is true with the wife's call to *submit*. If someone you know comes to you and simply says, "I want you to submit!" (We know people don't really talk like this, but let's pretend they did). Maybe if you trusted the person you would answer with an awkward, "OK...but what am I submitting to?" Telling someone to *submit* without telling them what they are to submit *to* is meaningless.

In many ways, the wife's calling hinges on who her husband is, what he holds as his compelling vision of success. She is called to submit to *him*. Who is he? She is called to help *him* succeed. With what? What mission is she being asked to help with? Many men have the "dime-a-dozen" vision of success. If you ask these men to describe success they will say something like this:

> "My vision of success is that we will have a nice family. We will get along, and have some kids. We will get a house and a couple of cars. We will take some vacations, be involved in our church, and try to make a difference in our community. We will grow old together, and enjoy our grandchildren. And, well, that's it. That's success!"

Men, there are a couple problems with the "dime-a-dozen" vision. First, your wife can find 999 other men who have this exact same mission and vision for their lives. There is nothing special about it. Second, it is simply not compelling enough for your wife to want to give her heart and soul to *helping* you succeed.

A Compelling Vision

So if that is not the vision of success, what is? What does it take to have a dynamically Christ-centered, Bible-driven, visionary marriage? It begins with a husband who has a dynamically Christ-centered, Bible-driven, multi-generational vision for his life. This sort of marriage launches when a husband comes to his wife and says,

98 | *Visionary Marriage*

"Let me tell you why I think God created me. Let me tell you why I think He has brought me to this point in my life, and where He wants me to go from here. I believe God created me to glorify Him first and foremost through loving you. He created me to love you, serve you, and encourage faith in you. I am convinced that God wants to use our marriage to further His Kingdom. If God would then give us children, it is the mission of my life to impress their hearts with a love for God, equip them in the world to make a difference for Christ, and ultimately to help them get safely home to their Father in Heaven. I want to see our children raise our grandchildren to know and love God, and that God would use our descendents to impact the whole world for Him. This is the main reason why I believe God made me, and the primary mission that He has given me. Will you help me succeed?"

It begins with a husband who has a dynamically Christ-centered, Bible-driven, multi-generational vision for his life.

The heart of the Christian woman shouts, "Yes!" Now, they are no longer two but one. The distinct, God-given roles of husband and wife combine together for a Christian purpose—the spiritual transformation of one another, and the raising of godly children. When a couple shares the same compelling Christian mission, that mission directs their decisions and enables them to endure hardship. They know that they are not together by chance, but they have been joined together by God for purposes far greater than themselves. In the chapters ahead we will talk practically about how husband and wife can help each other grow spiritually, and how to build a marriage with multi-generational vision.

Prayer:

Dear God,

You created marriage and family to bless us, transform us, and impact the world. You created my marriage and family to bless, transform, and impact as well. Because of that, I know that the enemy has been and will continue to tempt us, distract us, and attack us. Your Word tells us that You call husbands and wives to leave, cleave, and become one. That is what I want for our marriage. I don't want to be glorified roommates. I don't want to focus on our individual lives. I want what You want: for us to be no longer two, but one. I know that will take both of us embracing and committing ourselves to the roles You have given us. Help me "turn my key" and then pray and do everything I can to encourage my spouse to do the same.

In Jesus' name, Amen

Questions for further thought and discussion

1. In your marriage, how have you done in the three stages of leaving, cleaving, and becoming one? What aspects of this have you done well? Where have you fallen short?

2. Can you think of situations in your marriage where you have been in "blame mode?" How effective was that approach?

3. In this chapter, we challenged you to "turn your key" and not wait for your spouse. Name something specific that you could do this week to embrace your biblical calling as husband or wife.

4. What new insights did you gain about how to bring together the job descriptions of husband and wife?

CHAPTER 11

The Mission of Spiritual Transformation

Why Did You Get Married?

These were the opening questions in Visionary Marriage. Why did you get married? Why are you still married? These are questions of purpose and mission. God created the institution of marriage with specific purposes in mind, and He wants you to know those purposes and to give your best to fulfilling them. Understanding God's purpose for marriage is essential if you want to shift your relationship from that of glorified roommates toward a visionary marriage for the glory of God. In this chapter we will look at the first shared mission for marriage; the mission of spiritual transformation.

The Great Commission Starts at Home

After Jesus was raised from the dead, He gave His disciples their marching orders. We call it the Great Commission.

> *Therefore go and make disciples of all nations, baptizing them in the name of the Father and of the Son and of the Holy Spirit, and teaching them to obey everything I have commanded you. And surely I am with you always, to the very end of the age.*

MATTHEW 28:19-20

Jesus gives one imperative command in this text, "make disciples." Introduce people to Christ. Help them grow in Christ. Equip them to make a difference for Christ in the lives of others. Evangelism, discipleship, baptism, teaching, and equipping all fall under this one command, "make disciples." If you are married, this call to discipleship begins with the soul of your spouse. God wants you to do all in your power to encourage repentance and faith in those around you, and who is nearer to you than your husband or your wife?

Do you remember what the ultimate purpose of the husband is, according to Ephesians 5?

Husbands, love your wives, just as Christ loved the church and gave himself up for her to make her holy, cleansing her by the washing with water through the word...

EPHESIANS 5:25-26

A husband is called to first love and serve his wife, so that he might ultimately encourage faith in her heart, and lead her to be the noble woman God created her to be. The Christian husband understands that the most important life-mission God has given him is encouraging spiritual growth and transformation in his wife.

If you are married, this call to discipleship begins with the soul of your spouse.

Do you remember the first role God gave to wives in Genesis 2? God said it was not good for the man to be alone, and so He made a *helper* fit for him. This noble calling of helper applies to many areas of marriage and family life, but there is one area of *helping* that is more important than any other. Ladies, for what ultimate purpose did God create your husband? He created your husband for the same reason He created everyone, to bring Him glory!

Everyone who is called by my name, whom I created for my glory, whom I formed and made…

ISAIAH 43:7

Your husband was created to glorify God! He was created so that when people look at him, they would see Christ in and through him. This same God, who created your husband for His glory, saw fit to create for him a wife to help him become a godly man.

The mission of your marriage is not about *you*. Perhaps you have heard someone describe the Christian life as "others-centered." If you are married, the first "other" to be centered on is your spouse. Husbands, the mission of spiritual transformation begins with your ministry to your wife. Wives, the mission of spiritual transformation begins with your ministry to your husband. If you have not read the excellent marriage book from Gary Thomas, entitled *Sacred Marriage*, we recommend it to you.[19] Right on the cover of the book, Thomas poses this powerful question, "What if God created marriage to make us holy, more than to make us happy?" We are not down on happiness as a goal of marriage, but God created marriage for an even greater purpose than earthly happiness…eternal holiness.

Your Family—The Ultimate Discipleship Small Group

There is a lot of buzz in the church today about discipleship small groups. They go by lots of names. Community groups. Fellowship groups. Home groups. Cell groups. Pastors are going to conferences around the country where they learn foundations for successful small group ministry. Maybe you have heard some of these phrases being passed around your church:

"Discipleship happens in the context of relationships."

"We need to get back to authentic Christian community."

"Spiritual growth happens when we get real with one another."

The good news is that God believes in discipleship small groups too! He just has another name for them. He calls them families. God created the family as the *primary* place where discipleship would happen in the context of relationships, where we would find authentic Christian community, and where spiritual growth happens when we get real with one another. Are you looking for *authentic* relationships? Just go home. We are quite confident that there you will find all the authenticity you want.

The truth is that who we are at home is who we really are. Who your spouse is at home reveals his or her true character and nature. Who your children are at home is the *real* child. How many famous people have one public image, but were totally different people behind the scenes? Who was the *real* Tiger Woods? The guy on the TV and magazine covers, or the one sneaking out on his wife?

In our judgment, one of the reasons churches are feeling such an intense need for discipleship small groups within the church is that families are no longer functioning as the primary place of spiritual growth and accountability. Rather **The truth is that** than focus their primary energies on help- **who we are at** ing Christian families function as dynamic **home is who we** discipleship centers, churches can uninten- **really are.** tionally raise up a surrogate discipleship structure which is far less effective.[20]

Consider how perfectly God designed the spiritually-transforming power of the family, and particularly the marriage relationship. The family in general (and marriage in particular) is like a crucible. A crucible is a ceramic pot into which impure metal is placed. The crucible is then superheated, and the impurities in the metal rise to the surface and can be removed. The only way to get the impurities to separate from the precious metal is under intense heat.

In the same way, only family relationships are hot enough to bring out the worst in your character! Have you ever wondered why the worst of you comes out at home? Thankfully, the intensity of family life also brings out the best in us as well! But consider the other side for a moment. Have you ever given your boss the silent treatment? Imagine that you are going about your job, and your supervisor comes up to you and asks if he can talk with you for a moment. You totally ignore him. You simply pretend he is not there. Would you ever do such a thing? Probably not. If you did, your pink slip would not be far behind. We would never give the silent treatment to our boss. Instead, we reserve that sort of rude behavior for our loved ones, particularly our spouse.

Some people don't like this reality that family and marriage function as a crucible in our lives. It isn't right that we treat strangers better than we treat our own family members. While this is often true, it isn't right, and it isn't good. Consider with us the beauty and perfection that God built into family life. God created family and marriage as the most intense and personal of all human relationships, so that the worst of your character (and the best!) would come out with the people that God created to love you unconditionally for the rest of your life and help you become more like Christ. It is a perfect plan…except for the fact that we don't understand that this *is* the plan. It is not an accident that the worst parts of your spouse's character come out in the marriage relationship. God built marriage this way so that you could succeed in your shared mission of helping each other become more like Christ.

Will You Allow God to Use Your Spouse to Transform You?

Do you sin daily? With all due respect, if you don't think you sin daily, your own heart has deceived you. Expect your spouse to sin daily as well. When your husband or wife sins, demonstrates poor character, or uses bad judgment, that is your opportunity to help him or her grow, not rub their nose in it. Your spouse's failures are God-given opportunities for you to engage in the together-mission of spiritual transformation.

The question is whether or not you will allow God to use your spouse to transform your character. Many Christians are more willing to be shaped, encouraged, and challenged by friends at church than they are by their husband or wife. Christian men often meet for Bible studies before work, or may even meet with a small group of accountability partners. If one of those men see an area of sin in your life, and they lovingly call you on it, you most likely will listen respectfully to what they are saying, and may even be willing to accept prayer and accountability toward change. But what would you do if your wife brought up the exact same concern, using the exact same words? Would you allow your friends to challenge and shape you, but reject your wife? Women frequently do the same thing. Groups of Christian women will meet at church or in homes for prayer and Bible study. Ladies, if the women in your prayer group lovingly expressed their concern to you that you may not be as frugal as you should be with your money, you would likely listen respectfully to what they were saying, and might even accept prayer and ongoing encouragement toward change. But what if your husband shared the same concern using the same words? Would you be equally receptive?

Your spouse's failures are God-given opportunities for you to engage in the together-mission of spiritual transformation.

Many married Christians have replaced God's primary and most powerful discipleship relationship in our lives (our relationship with our spouse) with surrogate relationships which are far less personal, less effective, but more easily managed. You can fool your small group. You can't fool your spouse. Our prayer is that you will choose to allow God to use your spouse, more than anyone else in your life, to help you become more like Christ. In the next chapter, we will talk about practical ways that a husband can encourage faith in his wife, and how a wife can encourage her husband to be a more godly man.

Prayer:

Dear God,

I know You have united me to my spouse for a purpose. I know my marriage isn't about me. My mission begins with encouraging my spouse to become more like Jesus, to become the person You created him/her to be. I desperately need Your help in this calling. Not only do I need Your help in order to encourage faith in my husband/wife, but I need humility to receive challenge and encouragement from my spouse. It is much easier for me to receive feedback and challenge from others. Fill my heart with humility. Help me to listen to my spouse's concerns and take them seriously. Remind me every day that You created my spouse to help me become more like You.

In Jesus' name, Amen

Questions for further thought and discussion

1. How well is your family functioning as a discipleship center? In what ways do you help each other grow? In what ways are you resistant to each other?

2. Why, when most of us think of "Christian ministry," do we skip right past ministering to our spouse and think about others outside our home?

3. Can you think of a time that your spouse tried to bring one of your "growth areas" to your attention? How did you respond?

CHAPTER 12

How to Encourage Faith in Each Other

How a Husband Can Encourage Faith in His Wife

As we have learned, in Ephesians 5:25-26, God calls the husband to be a loving servant-leader to his wife. He is called by God to make her holy, to sanctify her. Where does a husband begin? How can a husband, who is a sinner himself, possibly hope to spiritually lead and influence his wife? Thankfully, God has not left us to our own devices and creativity. Not only does God give the *mission*, He gives us the *method*.

> *Husbands, love your wives, just as Christ loved the church and gave himself up for her to make her holy, cleansing her by the washing with water* **through the word**... *(bold mine)*

> Ephesians 5:25-26

How can a husband encourage spiritual growth in his wife? God gives him the place to start. A husband should take the lead in bringing the Bible into the marriage relationship. Men, invite your wife to read the Bible with you. If she won't do it, keep reading it on your own, and dedicate yourself to loving her and serving her. If your wife is a follower of Christ, and she feels safe with you, not only will she read the Bible with you, but she will love it (and love you for it).

Reading the Bible with Your Wife

Why read the Bible together? There are two big reasons. First, this is the method that God gives to husbands here in Ephesians. In many places in the Bible, God not only tells us *what* He wants us to do, but He tells us *how* to do it. Whenever God gives us the *method*, we should pay attention and get to work, trusting that He knows the best *way* to do what is right. Men, there is no need to get overly creative here. God says a husband can spiritually bless his wife by bringing the Bible into the relationship. Take His word for it. The second reason is that Scripture is powerful. Your mission is to encourage faith in your wife. Where will the power come from for that spiritual transformation?

> *For the word of God is living and active, sharper than any two-edged sword, piercing to the division of soul and of spirit, of joints and of marrow, and discerning the thoughts and intentions of the heart.*
>
> Hebrews 4:12 ESV

When husband and wife open their hearts to God's Word and seek to submit their thoughts and choices to God's revealed will—spiritual transformation is not far behind. Men, the picture is not of you holding the Bible over your wife, challenging her to be a better Christian. Instead, a godly husband first holds the Bible over himself, submitting himself to its authority in every area of life, and then he humbly invites his wife to join him in submission to God.

Whenever God gives us the *method*, we should pay attention and get to work, trusting that He knows the best *way* to do what is right.

By God's grace, we are doing well in regularly reading the Bible together as a family, but we still have a long way to go in reading the Bible consistently as a couple. I (Rob) made a big mistake in the early years of our marriage when it came to Bible reading together. In my mind I pictured us doing "couples' devotions." I would spend personal time each day working through a passage of Scripture, while Amy was doing the same, and then later in the week we would come together for a rich hour of spiritual sharing and prayer. We would pour out all we had learned during the week, and all the ways God had changed us. Our individual growth would merge together into powerful marital growth! Well...it never exactly happened that way. Frankly, we were lucky if we made it past the one-week mark. I tried and failed at this plan a few times. Why was it so hard? It was because I was trying to take us from kindergarten to graduate school overnight. We were not reading the Bible together at all, and I thought that the place to start was with a full-blown, multi-faceted couples' devotional!

Husbands, God wants you to read the Bible with your wife because it is His first prescribed method of spiritual encouragement. Start small. Start somewhere. G.K. Chesterton astutely said, "If a thing is worth doing, it is worth doing poorly." Consider trying it this way. The first few times you do this, you can count on it being awkward. The awkwardness comes from the enemy. Fight through it! Just say, "Honey, I was wondering if you would sit down on the couch with me for a few minutes while I read the Bible." She may pass out, so give her a few minutes to come to. She will then **Husbands, God wants you to read the Bible with your wife because it is His first prescribed method of spiritual encouragement.** probably say, "Who are you, and what you have you done with my husband?" Laugh that off, and invite her again to join you. She will slowly move over to the couch, and cautiously sit down. Open your Bible to the first chapter of the Gospel of John, and read the first two or three paragraphs. It will take just a few minutes. When you are done reading, say to your wife, "Thank you, Dear." Your wife (continuing to wonder if you are really her husband) will reply in kind, "Uh, OK. Thanks…to you, too." At which point you can both get up and go back about your other business.

Will it really be that awkward? Probably…for the first few times. You will both have to push through the spiritual battle of reading the Bible together, and the only way to win the battle is to just do it. Don't feel like you need to have deep spiritual conversations when you first start. Just sit down together, and read a few paragraphs. Start somewhere. Start small. Watch what Jesus will do.

Praying with Your Wife

We need to apply the same principles of "start somewhere, start small" to the practice of praying together. I (Rob) made the same mistake in this area that I made with the goal of reading the Bible together. In my mind, I imagined dramatic, hour-long prayer meetings at the side of our bed. That would be wonderful! But a couple doesn't go from little or no prayer, to that kind of prayer overnight.

In our marriage, the time right before bed has proven to be the best time for us to pray together. However, there are other ways to do it. If you are not praying at all together right now, consider this simple way to get prayer moving in your marriage. It will take you less than 10 seconds each day. Can you spare that kind of time? Your "prayer point" is the moment that you reunite at the end of the day. For most couples that is somewhere between 5pm and 8pm. Whenever you or your wife walk in the door, and you are both home for the remainder of the evening, that is your moment. A lot of conflict happens when our worlds collide at the end of the day. She brings all her stress, and you bring all yours. That makes it a great moment to pray.

Let's say that you walk in the front door at 6:00 P.M. Make it your first move to find your wife, take her hand and ask her to pray with you. "Honey, can we pray together?" "Uh…sure, I guess." (She is still wondering what has happened to you.) "Dear

Lord, thanks for bringing us back together tonight. Bless our marriage and our family. In Jesus' name, amen."

That's it? Yes. That's it. Start somewhere. Start small. If you keep waiting around for when you have time for your hour-long prayer meeting, your prayer life will likely not move forward. Prayers do not have to be long to be powerful. When a husband initiates genuine prayer, God responds...and his wife responds, too!

Does this mean that the husband should always be the one to initiate prayer? Is it wrong for the wife to ask her husband to pray with her, or to remind him that they should take some time and pray together? I (Rob) am grateful that Amy regularly reminds me that we should stop and take time to pray. I wish that I was more consistent and dedicated to spiritual disciplines. It is a spiritual weakness in my life. God has given me Amy to *help me* grow as a man of God. I need her help, and I appreciate it. However, the *goal* is that the husband is regularly taking the lead and the initiation when it comes to spiritual practices in the home.

Praying for Your Wife

Men, we just talked about praying *with* your wife. Now let's talk about praying *for* your wife. You can pray for her when you are praying together, but you can also encourage faith and spiritual transformation in her by praying for her on your own. This was the first action step that God led me (Rob) to take after He turned my heart to my wife and my calling to love her, serve her, and lead her.

A couple mornings a week (I wish I could say it was every day) I would get up and spend a few moments thinking about the day that Amy had before her. What was she going to face? What would her challenges be? What needs did she have? I tried to identify something that Amy needed that day...something substantive. As a homeschooling mom with six children, there are many things she needs *every* day. She needs patience, wisdom, gentleness, and endurance. All these things come from God and God alone, so as her husband, as her spiritual head, I can actively pray for God to fill her with these things!

Once I had thought about Amy's day and identified a need she had, I would write her short note which went something like this:

> "Dear Amy, I was thinking about you this morning and praying for you. I know that with all you have going on today you are going to need lots of patience and peace. I prayed for you from Philippians 4:7, that God would give you His peace that passes all understanding. Know that I am praying for you today. I love you, Rob"

I would leave these notes out at her breakfast spot and wouldn't talk about them with her unless she brought it up. My purpose was to build her up through prayer and encouragement. It had a powerful affect on our relationship. I remember Amy saying to me, "I feel like your prayers for me are more powerful than my prayers for me!"

Lead the Way in Worship at Church

Christian men are "church men." They understand that God wants them to faithfully participate in the weekly worship gathering of their local church. There are no perfect men, and there are no perfect churches. Sadly, there seems to be an increasing number of people who have the attitude, "I love Jesus, but I don't like church." As if you can love Christ, but hate His bride! Men, if you want to bless and encourage your wife and family, take the lead on Sunday mornings. Get your clothes ready the night before. Help get things organized for the kids. Be the first one out of bed so you can get breakfast going. Make it your mission to have the Sabbath begin with peace in your home, not insanity!

Do your wife and children see you more excited about the big game on Sunday afternoon or worshipping God on Sunday morning? Don't think they aren't watching and learning what is really important to you. Ask God to make you a man who *loves* to worship Him and listen to the preaching of His Word. When a wife has to get the kids up, get her husband up, and crack the whip all morning in order to get the family to church close to on time—the family is spiritually upside down. Sabbath worship is a vital area of spiritual leadership for husbands. It is not a day to crack the whip, but to be Ephesians 5 men; loving, servant-leaders.

> **Men, if you want to bless and encourage your wife and family, take the lead on Sunday mornings.**

When you do finally arrive at church, be sure to sit together as a family. Don't encourage your children to sit with their friends, or send them off to children's ministry or youth ministry while you are in church. The church service is not an adult education hour. It is a gathering of the faith community in the presence of God under the authority of His Word. Your children are a part of that faith community, and if you are there, they belong by your side. The Bible isn't silent on this issue! Throughout the Old and New Testaments we see examples of children of all ages worshipping with their parents. [21]

Husbands bless and spiritually encourage their wives when they take the lead in making church a family priority. Men, if you are not eager to be in church yourself, ask God to change your heart. In the meantime, make church a priority because it is the right thing to do and because it is a vital component of your spiritual leadership of the family. [22]

How A Wife Can Help Her Husband Grow in Godly Character

God's first job description for a wife was *helper* to her husband. Wives, your husband's ultimate purpose is to glorify God. God created you, and brought you into your husband's life to help him succeed. Here are some ways you can do it.

Respond Positively to His Spiritual Leadership

We have known many husbands who have been deterred and discouraged from spiritual leadership in the home...by their Christian wives! Few Christian men today grew up in a home where they saw a visionary marriage between their parents. Even if your husband's father was a Christian, it is unlikely that his father took it upon himself to train your husband in what it meant to be a godly man. If your husband is making *any* attempt to be the loving, servant-leader of your home you are blessed!

Earlier in the book we talked about how vital it is to understand that the spiritual forces of evil seek to attack men with spiritual passivity. The enemy doesn't want your husband taking any active steps of spiritual leadership in the family. Look at the list of action steps for husbands earlier in this chapter. The enemy will do whatever it takes to prevent your husband from making any attempt to do them! He will be under attack from morning till night. If your husband fights through the spiritual attack, and however awkwardly initiates prayer, Bible reading, family worship, or prioritizing worship at church, that is a critical moment where he needs your encouragement.

> **If your husband is making *any* attempt to be the loving, servant-leader of your home you are blessed!**

Tragically, the enemy tempts wives to be critical of their husband's attempts at spiritual leadership. Sure, he tried to pray before dinner, but it was so short, and didn't seem that meaningful. Yes, he tried to bring the kids together for Bible reading, but then he was angry and impatient with them for not paying attention. Here is the short of it: Many Christian men are trying in their own small ways to spiritually engage with their wives and kids, but their wives don't feel as if it is good enough or that "he is not doing it the way I would." If your husband takes a step toward spiritual leadership, and you discourage him, it may be a long time before he tries again.

Wives, anytime you see your husband spiritually engage, go *way* out of your way to encourage him. Let's say that he awkwardly tries the "pray with you as soon as he gets home from work" suggestion above. As soon as he says, "amen," look into his eyes and say, "Thank you so much for doing that! There aren't very many men out there who would even think about praying with their wives when they come home at the end of a long day. I appreciate it!" He will walk away feeling affirmed and encouraged to try that again.

Praise him for godly decisions

Your husband makes dozens of decisions every day. Some of them will be noble and godly, others far less than that. There is certainly a time and place to talk with him about his unwise choices (we will talk about that below), but praising him for his right decisions will do far more to create more of those in the future, than nagging him continually about how he is messing up. Consider these two Proverbs.

If your husband takes a step toward spiritual leadership, and you discourage him, it may be a long time before he tries again.

> *It is better to live in a corner of the housetop, than in a house shared with a quarrelsome wife.*
>
> PROVERBS 21:9 ESV

> *It is better to live in a desert land than with a quarrelsome and fretful woman.*
>
> PROVERBS 21:19 ESV

Ladies, if you want your husband to withdraw from you, emotionally and physically, there is an easy way to do it. Be routinely critical, quarrelsome, and negative. He will avoid you like the plague. When he is physically around, his heart will be elsewhere, and you will feel as if you are talking to a wall.

Instead of harping on his sins (of which there will be many: remember, he is a sinner), make a plan to intentionally praise him for his right and godly choices. When he keeps his word by coming home on time, tell him that you appreciate it. When he handles a discipline situation with the kids with wisdom, tell him that he is a good dad. Be on the look-out for godly choices, big and small, and affirm him by pointing them out.

Use words and phrases that are particularly encouraging to men. Say, "I am proud of you." Tell him, "I believe in you." Let him know, "What you did made me happy." Affirm him by saying, "You are a good man." Obviously, don't say these things if they aren't coming from your heart. But if you are waiting for your husband to be perfect in every area of his life before you affirm him, you never will. It is far better to understand that you will help your husband become more Christ-like *by* affirming him everywhere you can.

When he makes right choices, tell him every way you can. Text him. Email him. Leave him a voice mail. Tell him face to face. Write him a note. I (Rob) can personally attest to the affirming power of notes. One of the things that Amy has done for me over the years is to write me short notes of affirmation. Many of them are tucked in the pages of my Bible. Some have been there for years. (One of them is even on red paper…the contents of which are not for sharing in public!) On those slips of paper are these phrases, "I believe in you," "I am proud of you," "You are a good man." I have read those notes hundreds of times. When I am anxious or feeling discouraged, I frequently pull out those notes. God uses those words to build me up. If God has given me a wife who believes in me, that's all I need.

Pray for Your Husband

Husbands can transform their wives through prayer, and wives can transform their husbands through prayer. Some of you may be thinking, "Come on! Can't you come up with anything more creative than 'pray for your husband?' I need something new." First, remember that our job is not to come up with creative methods to do the things God has called us to do. He wants us to do *what* He wants, the *way* He wants it done. Prayer is God's idea, not ours. When we want to see things change in our lives, particularly when we want to see others change, our first calling is to pray. Ultimately, God is the one who causes us to grow and to be sanctified. If God is the one who will change your spouse, then our job starts with prayer, asking Him to do just that.

In addition, for those of you who may be in the "Pray for my husband, yeah, yeah, yeah, what else?" camp, have you ever tried praying *consistently* for your husband? Many people who minimize prayer are the ones who haven't done it.

Wives, use prayer to bless your husband and to encourage spiritual transformation in him. Bless him by lifting his cares and concerns to God, praying for God to give him favor and success in all he does. Pray for God to bless him at work and bless him financially. Pray for God to give him opportunities to share Christ with others and to be generous. Identify one or two key growth areas in his life, and pray specifically for the Holy Spirit to bring about transformation in those areas. I (Amy) prayed for many years for Rob to catch a vision for his role as spiritual leader of our home. God answered that prayer.

> **Many people who minimize prayer are the ones who haven't done it.**

Spiritual Challenge: One to Another

While there are specific things that wives and husbands can do to encourage faith in each other, there is a calling that both husband and wife share—to lovingly and respectfully let the other person know when they are not acting in a godly manner.

If husband and wife are *both* believers, then a vital part of how they fulfill their shared mission of spiritual transformation is by practicing Jesus' teaching found in Matthew 18.

> *"If your brother sins against you, go and tell him his fault, between you and him alone. If he listens to you, you have gained your brother."*
>
> MATTHEW 18:15 ESV

We make a big mistake when we read the Bible and fail to apply biblical principles for *Christian* relationships to our *marriage* relationship. Is not your wife your sister in Christ? Is not your husband your brother in Christ? Whenever we see instructions for Christian community and fellowship, we should apply them first to our family members, beginning with our spouse.[23]

If you are going to fulfill the mission that God has given you to help your spouse grow in godliness, you will need to lovingly and respectfully confront sin, mistakes, and unwise choices. You are not the Holy Spirit, but the Holy Spirit will use you more than anyone else in your spouse's life to convict them of their sin, and help them repent, and turn toward righteousness.

The challenge here is not so much in expressing your concerns to your spouse about his or her struggles with sin and poor choices, but *how* to do it. Pointing out someone's faults is easy. Helping someone admit their faults and helping them grow through them is far more challenging. Here are two things to keep in mind when you need to express concern to your husband or wife about a sinful or unhealthy pattern.

Forgive as the Lord forgave you

Before you go and talk with your spouse, take some time and remember how gracious God has been to you through Jesus

Christ. Remember that God, through the sacrifice of His son, has offered forgiveness to you for all the sins you have committed, and will commit, against Him. Because you have been forgiven, He calls you to be ready to forgive as well. Enter into the conversation with your spouse with a humble spirit, knowing that you have been forgiven much.

Speak with Grace and Truth

One of the marks of Jesus' ministry was that He was always filled with grace and truth. He gave maximum grace, and maximum truth. One never watered down the other. This is the ultimate challenge when you need to confront your spouse. How can you communicate maximum grace? How can you communicate maximum truth? We communicate maximum grace when we affirm our commitment to the person and to the marriage. We communicate maximum grace when we are clear that we will not stop loving the other person and that we are having this conversation because of how much we value them. We communicate maximum truth, when we speak plainly and simply about our concerns. You may even want to get out a sheet of paper and on the left side of the page write down all the things you can say to your spouse to communicate grace for them and grace for the situation. On the right side of the page write down the things you need to say in order to speak the truth about your concerns.

Be Prepared for Change

If you are serious about allowing God to use your spouse to shape your character, be prepared to become a more godly person!

I (Rob) have noticed that as I have grown in my faith, my sensitivity to sin has increased. God used Amy to help me grow in an important area of my spiritual life. I had a pattern of watching TV shows which were not building up my faith and character. The

Bible has a lot to say about our thought life, and what we allow ourselves to watch and listen to.

> *Finally, brothers, whatever is true, whatever is noble, whatever is right, whatever is pure, whatever is lovely, whatever is admirable—if anything is excellent or praiseworthy—think about such things.*
>
> PHILIPPIANS 4:8

I was not being as thoughtful as I should have been about my media choices. Seinfeld, Lost, and 24 were among my favorites. Are these the most perverse and violent shows on TV? No. But would I watch any of them with risen and majestic Jesus sitting on the couch next to me? No way.

If you are serious about allowing God to use your spouse to shape your character, be prepared to become a more godly person!

Not only did I watch them, but I was a little addicted to them. I knew the schedule. I taped the shows I couldn't watch in order to see them later. Lost and 24 were particularly addicting. Amy was marvelously godly in how she encouraged me to address this area of my life. The first thing she did, as God began to convict her about this, was that she stopped watching with me. She didn't make a big deal about it or rub it in my face. She just chose not to watch. She later began to express to me some of the reasons that *she* chose to change her habits. I could see what was going on. She then began to gently challenge me about my choice to keep watching. She respectfully asked me, "Would you be proud to watch this with our kids someday?" That was the one that really got me. The Holy Spirit used her gracious and truthful encouragement to convict me and turn my heart toward taking this area of purity in my life more seriously.

God used Rob to help me (Amy) grow in an important area of my parenting. Sometimes I can use a harsh or critical tone with the kids. I often have no idea I sound the way I do. I have learned that one of the most powerful influences in a home is the tone of voice that family members use with one another. As a wife and mother, my tone often sets the tone for everyone else. Rob has helped me grow in this area. First, he took the lead in talking about the importance of tone of voice in the family. He wasn't heavy-handed or accusatory about it. In fact, he makes a concerted effort to focus on the tone that he uses with me and the kids in order to set a good example. We all fail in this area, but Rob really gives it his best.

When my tone becomes harsh or critical, he will gently challenge me, "Honey, remember your tone of voice." It doesn't come across as criticism, but appropriate encouragement. The Holy Spirit is using Rob to convict me and turn my heart toward taking this area of holiness in my life more seriously.

One Thing at a Time, Please

Have you ever given your spouse the entire laundry list of your complaints, criticisms, and disappointments? Most of us have done it at one time or another. We lose our temper, and then we let loose. The results are never productive.

Imagine sitting down with your boss for your annual review. He tells you that in the year ahead he would like for you to work on twenty-three areas of improvement. How will you feel? Deflated, discouraged, and hopeless! Even if he is right, that there are twenty-three areas in which you need to improve, you can't possibly make progress in every area all in one year.

Because your spouse is an expert sinner, he or she has far more than twenty-three growth areas. But if you are going to embrace the shared mission of spiritual transformation, you would be wise to ask the Lord to show you one or two that you can focus on in the coming months. Ask God to give you grace, patience, and understanding with the rest of the list.

Prepare to Launch

Are you both ready to turn your keys? The first shared mission of marriage is the spiritual transformation of your spouse. For the husband, the mission begins with his ministry to his wife. For the wife, the mission begins with her ministry to her husband. As we will see in the next chapter, the end purpose is not two spiritual-transformed individuals with a nice marriage. Marriage isn't about the two of you…happily ever after. It is not just about you…it's about them. We now turn our attention to the second shared mission of marriage, raising godly children, grandchildren, and beyond.

Prayer:

Dear God,

Thank You that You created marriage for a reason. Thank You for creating husbands and wives with different roles, but for a common purpose. I want to please You in my role as husband/wife. I want to do everything in my power to gracefully and truthfully help my spouse to become more like Christ. I need Your help to do it. Help me to not focus on new creative ways to do this, but rather follow the direction You have already given to me in Your Word. I pray for my husband/wife right now. Transform his/her character into the character of Christ. Use me to accomplish Your purposes in his/her life.

In Jesus' name, Amen

Questions for further thought and discussion

1. Have you ever tried to give your spouse constructive criticism? How did you do it? What was the result?

2. What practical steps could you take to increase your prayer life together as a couple?

3. Which is harder for you? Speaking with grace or truth? Why? How could you improve your skill at maximizing both?

CHAPTER 13

The Mission of Raising Godly Children

Throughout *Visionary Marriage* we have not shied away from talking about a biblical vision for marriage, even if that vision goes against the culture around us. These final two chapters will be no different, and may in fact be the most challenging of all.

As we considered the first shared mission of marriage, the mission of spiritual transformation, we learned that the focus of the marriage relationship should not be on us as individuals, but on our spouse. The husband's mission begins with the soul of his wife. The wife's mission begins with the soul of her husband. As God takes two people and makes them one in marriage, He gives them a together-mission, which goes beyond the marriage, and extends for generations to come. This second mission of marriage is the raising of godly children. The husband focuses on the wife's spiritual transformation. The wife focuses on her husband's spiritual transformation. Together, husband and wife give themselves to their most important ministry—the spiritual transformation of their children.

Earlier we looked at the silence in many churches regarding the plain biblical teaching about the role and calling of women in marriage and in the home. This issue, having children and raising them for the glory of God, is even more culturally explosive, and as a result is often a subject that is untouched from our pulpits. As with every other matter raised in this book, we are faced with a question when it comes to the topic of children, do we believe the Bible is enough to shape our convictions and decisions, or do we need to rely more on our experience and intuition? [24]

How Many, How Soon?

In some ways we feel as if we are attempting the impossible here. Our culture has undergone a radical revolution in how children are viewed and welcomed into the world. Tragically, many believers in the church today view the mission of raising godly children through the same lenses as the culture around us, and don't even know it. This was the case for us when we got married.

This issue, having children and raising them for the glory of God, is even more culturally explosive, and as a result is often a subject that is untouched from our pulpits.

When you were engaged, did anyone ever ask you, "How many, how soon?" It is a common question. In other words, "How many children do you want to have, and when do you want to start?" We were not exactly on the same page with the number. Amy usually said, "No less than three, no more than four." Rob said, "Three." However, when it came to the timetable, we were on the same page. We wanted to wait three years. We both *felt* as if that was a good amount of time for us to get our marriage on a solid footing. It was a priority to have time just for us. We now look back on this decision with some regret.

The decisions to get married and to have children are perhaps the two biggest decisions, next to trusting Christ, which a person makes in life. We both trusted Christ as children, so we went through our time of dating, engagement, and early marriage as believers. Yet, we didn't approach this big decision about children *as* Christians.

Christian Decision Making

How do Christians make big decisions? Will you go to college? If so, where will you go? Will you get married? Is he or she the one? Will you take that new job? If you are a Christian, how do you go about making big decisions like these? There are a few things Christians do to discern God's will. We pray and take the matter to the Lord. We pray things such as, "Lord, I don't want to make this decision in my own wisdom. I don't want my opinion to be the determining factor here. I want to do what You want me to do. Please show me Your will. Make it clear to me, and I will obey You." Along with prayer, we should eagerly search the Scriptures to learn all God has said about that particular issue in His Word. God has spoken on every matter of importance in the Bible, and we want to start there for truth and guidance. In addition to prayer, and submitting our thoughts to Scripture, we seek godly counsel. We share the big decision we are facing with other believers who we respect. We ask them for their prayers and advice. Over a period of time, through prayer, Scripture, and wise counsel we come to our decision.

We made many of our important decisions according to these Christian principles. Yet, when it came to this supremely important issue of "how many, how soon," we immediately responded, "Three or four, starting in three years." There was no prayer. There was no searching the Scriptures for all that the Lord had to tell us about having babies. There was no wise counsel.

We didn't realize until many years later, even though we were Christians, when it came to this vital area of our lives, we thought exactly like the rest of the world. We viewed the decision to have children as one we were in control of—100%. This was our call. How many? We decide. How soon? We decide.

It never even dawned on us that as Christians, we should seek God's will for us rather than our own! We never prayed, "God, when it comes to children, not our will, but Yours be done." We never opened the Bible to search for the direction that God has

We viewed the decision to have children as one we were in control of—100%. already given us about this vital mission of our marriage. We never sought godly counsel from people who knew the Bible. The decision about having children was ours...and ours alone. God's will and His divine revelation were not part of the equation. This was one of the many areas in our marriage where we discovered many years later that we had built our relationship on a broken foundation. We wish we could turn back the clock.

Four Life Connections

Part of developing and maintaining a Christian view of the world is keeping the right things connected in the right way. Consider the following diagram. Here are four things that God wants us to keep connected, and therefore four things that Satan wants to separate.

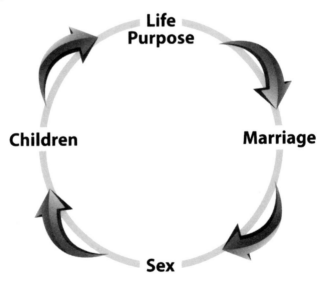

Let's start in the upper right of the cycle. Throughout this book, we have been encouraging you to keep your life purpose and your marriage connected. If you are married, your life purpose and calling begin with your spouse! Your first life purpose is not your job. Your first life purpose is not your volunteer work at church. As a married person, your most important life purpose is your ministry to and with your spouse. Satan wants to break that connection. He wants you to give your heart and soul first to work, friends, hobbies, and even noble things such as church, so that you will neglect the most important calling God has given you.

There are two basic paradigms for how to organize your life as it relates to career and family. You can wrap and flex family around your primary mission of career, or you can wrap and flex career around your primary mission of family. Our default setting is to wrap family around career. Family gives, family flexes, family sacrifices for the primary mission of career. Unless you make a *missional* Christian decision to change your paradigm to a family-centered mission, you will automatically live in the default paradigm. This is not to say that our work is not important in our lifelong calling to glorify God and point others toward Him. Rather, it is understanding that our Christian mission *begins* at home. If we win at work, but lose at home, we lose.

You can wrap and flex family around your primary mission of career, or you can wrap and flex career around your primary mission of family.

This principle is especially vital for men to understand in their role of provider. Sometimes Christian men are called to serve God in the military. But if a soldier is deployed and wins on the battlefield, but neglects the nurture of his wife from across the miles, he loses. Sometimes the demands of business require extensive travel. But if a business man closes the big deal after 3 months of being on the road, and at the same time loses the hearts of his children, he loses. God would have him win on both fronts, by having his heart rightly ordered!

The paradigm shift is not simply about time and strategy. It is heart issue. One man may be home a lot, but his heart may not be engaged in his mission there, and as a result he is not fulfilling God's purpose. Another man may be away from home more than he would like but because his heart is with his family first, God grants him success at home and beyond.

Satan also seeks to break the next connection. He is doing everything he can to break the link between marriage and sex. Our culture encourages us to have sex before marriage, outside of marriage, with ourselves, and with those of the same sex. Satan and the world call us to be sexual anywhere and everywhere *except* within monogamous, heterosexual marriage. God created the marvelous gift of sex for three reasons:

• To unite the spirit of husband and wife
• Bringing children into the world
• Pleasure for husband and wife

Notice how the enemy has perverted God's purposes for sex. He hasn't changed the definition, but rather has simply eliminated the first two, leaving pleasure…and pleasure alone. Sex for uniting the spirits of husband and wife? Sex for bringing children into the world? Don't be ridiculous. Sex is all about pleasure. That's it. That is Satan's lie.

Let's keep moving around the circle. God wants us to connect our life purpose with marriage, and marriage with sex. God also wants us to connect sex and children. It seems crazy to say this, but as we work with engaged couples we have to directly encourage them to keep the idea of sex and having babies together in their minds. The enemy has won a great victory! Unlike the men and women for the centuries before us, we now think about sex in one category, and having children in a totally separate category, as if sex and babies didn't have anything to do with each other.

Let's complete the circle. God wants you to see your life mission connected to your marriage, which is connected with sex, which is connected to having children, and then children become part of your life purpose. God has not brought you together in marriage just for you! God has brought you together for the sake of your children, grandchildren, and beyond.

The First Commandment

We have spent considerable time talking about God's vision for marriage from Genesis, chapters two and three. But even before the call from God to leave, cleave, and become one, the Lord gives man and woman the "big picture" vision for their marriage. Consider the very first words God spoke to the man and the woman after they had been created.

Unlike the men and women for the centuries before us, we now think about sex in one category, and having children in a totally separate category, as if sex and babies didn't have anything to do with each other.

> *And God blessed them. And God said to them, "Be fruitful and multiply and fill the earth and subdue it and have dominion over the fish of the sea and over the birds of the heavens and over every living thing that moves on the earth."*
>
> GENESIS 1:28 ESV

When was the last time your pastor preached on God's very first words to human beings? God makes Adam and Eve as husband and wife, and he immediately gives them a multi-generational mission. Be fruitful, multiply, fill the earth, and subdue it. God invites husband and wife into the miracle of creation. Here we find God's primary plan of global evangelism. The Lord wants the earth filled with worship and with His worshippers.

At this point, some might say, "Well, I think that we have done a pretty good job of filling the earth. In fact, the earth is too full! We need fewer people, not more people." Forgive our bluntness on this issue, but this is a lie which comes directly from an atheistic, evolutionary worldview and a socialist/communist political position. Not only does the myth of overpopulation come from the radical left, but it is totally unsupported by the numbers. Did you know the entire population of the earth could fit into the state of Texas, and every person would have 1,090 square feet all to themselves? There may be particular parts of the world that are overcrowded, but it is untrue to say that the earth is overpopulated, or that there are insufficient resources to meet people's needs. It is true that there are places in the world where repressive governments prevent the resources from getting to people in need. Most of us who grew up in the US and its government school system were indoctrinated with the myth of overpopulation. If you want to dig deeper into this issue, consider watching the new DVD documentary *Demographic Winter*.[25] Are you concerned about the crises facing the world such as poverty, hunger, and injustice? Do you know what we need more than anything else to address these problems? We need more people who love Jesus Christ and who are willing to lay down their lives for Him. By raising godly children, you can have a greater impact on the world than you can possibly imagine.

Unless the Lord Builds the House

Psalm 127 contains a powerful message, but many people miss it all together. This psalm is a short poem containing only five verses. Yet it is rarely preached or taught as a single unit. Rather, people take the first two verses and apply them totally out of context with the remainder of the psalm. Here are the first two verses. The words may be familiar to you:

> *Unless the Lord builds the house, its builders labor in vain. Unless the Lord watches over the city, the watchmen stand guard in vain. In vain you rise early and stay up later, toiling for food to eat for he grants sleep to those he loves.*
>
> Psalm 127:1-2

"Unless the Lord builds the house, its builders labor in vain." It is a fairly well-known passage from the Bible. Unfortunately, it is often preached as a stand-alone line without paying any attention to the entire subject matter of the psalm. This verse is ripped out of context and Christians are told something along the lines of, "If you plan your life apart from God, you are wasting your time. You need to build your family, your business, and your future on the sure foundation of God." Such teaching is certainly true, but Psalm 127:1 is not some general message of trusting God and including Him in your plans. Remember, this psalm only contains five verses. It is one unit, and was never intended to be separated into disjointed sections. Here are the final three verses:

Sons are a heritage from the Lord, children a reward from him. Like arrows in the hands of a warrior are sons born in one's youth. Blessed is the man whose quiver is full of them. They will not be put to shame when they contend with their enemies in the gate.

PSALM 127:3-5

What is God speaking about in Psalm 127? The blessing, reward, and Kingdom impact of children…many children! God says that sons are a heritage. God says that children are a reward. We pray that God's grace will work in the hearts of our six children with such power that when they leave our home they will be like spiritual arrows entering into the battle for Christ and for His Kingdom. God says a man is blessed when the house is filled with kids! The spirit of the world disagrees. Two kids should be enough for everyone. If however, you have two of the same gender, you have "permission" to try one more time.

Let's go back to verse 1. Unless the Lord builds the house, its laborers labor in vain. What is God saying? The call of this psalm is to allow God to build your family according to His plans, rather than yours. We know God is sovereign over all things in our lives, so second-guessing is not a very fruitful exercise. But we sometimes think about *who* is not a part of our family by intentionally avoiding children for the first three years of our marriage. Each of our six children truly is a blessing from God. We don't want to send any one of them back! To think God had more "blessings" in store for us that we intentionally avoided is more than a little depressing.

God says that a man is blessed when the house is filled with kids! The spirit of the world disagrees.

In some ways, waiting to have children is like continuing to watch the previews without ever getting to the feature presentation. You show up at the theater to see the big movie that has just been released. The ticket says the show starts at 7:00 P.M. You are in your seat and ready to go. At 7:00 P.M. the previews start. That one looks pretty good. No way am I going to that one. Three previews go past. Six previews go past. Come on already! You didn't come to see endless previews, you came to see the feature film. We look back at our three years before children, like the previews at the movies. It wasn't a bad time, but we had no idea that we were delaying the *best* while holding on to the *good*. We didn't realize we were delaying the most challenging, joyous, and important Christian mission of our lives.

The Rewards of Following God

Think about your response to this question, "What are the rewards for following God?" If a friend asked you this question, what would you say? Perhaps the first things that come to mind would include salvation, forgiveness, love, joy, peace, and wisdom. The list could go on and on. The rewards of following God are wonderful. Think about these rewards for a moment. Look at the short list we suggested. Are there any of these things you don't want? No way. Are there any of these things you want partially? Do we say, "God I really want you to forgive me, but I would only like 50% of your forgiveness?" Of course not! Would you like any of God's rewards delayed? No one tells God, "Lord, I really want to experience your joy and wisdom, but I'd like you to wait a few years before you give them to me." When it comes to the rewards of God, we want *all* of them, we don't want them in partial form, and we want them as soon as God will give them to us. Amen! So do we really believe Psalm 127:3, "Children are a *reward* from Him?" Children were the one reward from God that we wanted to delay, to limit, and to control.

Children and childbearing in the Bible are always viewed positively. God wants us to eagerly desire children, because our greatest impact in the world for Christ will likely be through them.

The Purpose of Unity

We have spent a lot of time in this book developing the biblical vision of marital unity…no longer two, but one. God has called you, as husband and wife, to be one in spirit, heart, mind and mission. This unity is not just for your enjoyment, it is a vital part of God's plan to impress the hearts of the next generation with a love for Him.

In Malachi 2 we find a dramatic text on how seriously God takes unity in marriage. In fact, God tells us something that He hates. In Malachi 2:16 we read, "God hates divorce." I (Rob) know all too well the pain and tragedy of divorce, as it has multiplied itself in my family tree. Yes, God hates divorce, but have you ever asked yourself *why* He hates it? Like Psalm 127, Christians often rip Malachi 2:16 out of its proper context. The oft quoted phrase, "God hates divorce," comes at the end of an important paragraph. In that paragraph, God explains *why* divorce is so serious.

> *You flood the LORD's altar with tears. You weep and wail because he no longer pays attention to your offerings or accepts them with pleasure from your hands. You ask, "Why?" It is because the LORD is acting as the witness between you and the wife of your youth, because you have broken faith with her, though she is your partner, the wife of your marriage covenant.*

Has not the LORD made them one? In flesh and spirit they are his. And why one?

MALACHI 2:13-15A

Here is the central question that God presses us to consider. From the beginning of Scripture, God calls husband and wife to unity. Here is the vital question. Why one? Why is this whole thing about husband and wife leaving, cleaving, and becoming *one* such a big deal to God? Here is God's answer.

And why one? **Because he was seeking godly offspring** *(Bold ours). So guard yourself in your spirit, and do not break faith with the wife of your youth. "I hate divorce," says the LORD God of Israel...*

MALACHI 2:15B-16A

Why is God so intent on you and your spouse becoming one? Because the Lord wants your children to love Him with all their hearts! When husband and wife are one in Christ, children have the best opportunity to follow Christ as well. So why is divorce such a big deal to God? Satan loves to use divorce to rob faith from children. If Satan can destroy a marriage *and* pull kids away from God, he has hit a home run. Malachi 2 is a powerful passage where God calls us to keep our vision for marital unity and the mission of having and raising godly children together.

What we are *not* saying

The point here is not that all good Christians have lots of kids, or that if you don't have children or have a small family that you are unspiritual. We have friends who have lost many children due to miscarriages (praise God those babies are safe with their Heavenly Father). Others are called to the ministry of adoption and foster care. You may be in a season where your primary investment in the next generation will be in the lives of your nieces and nephews, or in the lives of children at church. Perhaps you have never been able to have children. This is a deep grief that can only be understood by those who have experienced it. God is the One who opens and closes the womb. If this is your situation, continue to trust God. Trust His sovereignty. Bring Him glory every day through your faithfulness.

We are also not saying that you should be trying to get pregnant every time you have sex. This is not a chapter on the morality of birth control, although we strongly recommend that you carefully study the Scriptures on that issue. These two chapters on this controversial issue barely scratch the surface. For a very thoughtful discussion of these vital Christian issues, we recommend reading the book *Start Your Family* by Steve and Candace Watters.

Challenges and Encouragements

First, we challenge you to pray for God to give you an eager Christian love for children. Many of us have learned to view children negatively. Ask God to change your heart and give you an overwhelming desire for children and the opportunity to raise them for His glory.

Second, we encourage you to pray for the souls of the children, and perhaps grandchildren, that God has already blessed you with. Ask God to turn your heart to your children, and for Him to give you and your spouse a shared passion and shared vision for impressing their hearts with a love for God. Your marriage is not about *you*...it's about *them*. If you have children, do you have a plan to teach them about God and thoroughly equip them to live for Christ? We hope that after you finish *Visionary Marriage*, you will get a copy of *Visionary Parenting*, which will equip you with biblical vision and practical strategies to lead your kids and encourage you to do all in your power to prepare your children to follow God.[26]

Third, we hope you will take your future decisions about children to God in prayer. Are you willing to pray for His will, not yours? Are you willing to diligently search the Scriptures for all that God has said about having babies? Will God's Word be sufficient for you? Don't make these all-important decisions based solely on your experience, wisdom, and intuition.

Fourth, we challenge you to encourage an eager love for children in *your* children. Perhaps you are an empty-nest couple. Your kids are grown and gone. Encourage your grown children who are married to eagerly desire children, and do all in your power to help *them* raise your grandchildren for the glory of God. If you have the honor of being a grandparent, this is a prime ministry season of your life. Your impact and spiritual leadership in your family can now multiply into future generations!

Are you willing to pray for His will, not yours? Are you willing to diligently search the Scriptures for all that God has said about having babies?

In our final chapter ahead, we will expand the mission even further, and dream together about how God can use your marriage for His glory...even to the ends of the earth.

Prayer

Dear God,

Help us to take these all important decisions about having and raising children to You. We don't want to trust our own experience or instincts. Instead, help us to trust what You have revealed in Scripture. We live in an upside down culture which tells us that children are a burden, are too expensive, and that it is even irresponsible to have many children. We pray instead that You would give us an eager Christian love for children. If it is Your will, bless us with many children, grandchildren, and beyond...all for Your glory!

In Jesus' name, Amen.

Questions for further thought and discussion

1. Did people ever ask you before you were married, "How many? How soon?" What did you say? How did you come to that decision?

2. When you see a big family unloading from a van, or out to dinner, what thoughts cross your mind?

3. Do you believe that God can be trusted with the decision of whether or not to give you children? What would it look like to trust Him completely with this aspect of your life?

CHAPTER 14

A God-Sized
Vision

There are no perfect marriages, and there are no perfect families. However, God has seen fit to bring the two of you together into His gift of marriage. As we have been discovering throughout our journey together, God created marriage and family—your marriage and family—with a grand purpose. God has been working through families, imperfect families like yours, since the beginning of history to bring the message of salvation to the world. God, Himself, chose to enter the world as a member of a family. Consider the words from the nineteenth-century writer Jacob Abbott:

God has grouped men in families, having laid the foundation of this institution so deep in the very constitution of man that there has been no nation, no age, scarcely even a single savage tribe that has not been drawn to the result which He intended. For thousands of years, this institution has been assailed by every power that could shake it by violence from without, or undermine it by treachery from within. Lust and passion have risen in rebellion against it. Atheism has again and again advanced to the attack, but the Christian family unit stands unmoved. It has been indebted to no human power for its defense. It has needed no defense. The family stands on the firm, sure, and enduring foundation that God has made for it. Wars, famine, pestilence, and revolutions have swept over the face of society carrying confusion, terror, and distress to social struc-

tures. *Time has undermined and destroyed everything that it could touch, and all human institutions have thus been altered or destroyed in the lapse of ages. But the family lives on; it stands firm and unshaken. It survives every shock, and rises again unharmed after every tempest that blows over the social sky…God has laid its foundations too deep and strong to be removed.*[27]

A God-sized Vision

Do you remember the "dime-a-dozen" vision we talked about a few chapters ago? Get married. Have some kids. Buy a house. Be nice people. Take some trips. Enjoy grandkids. Our vision is too small! When we were first married, we had no idea how God's purposes for our marriage—the purposes of spiritual transformation and raising godly children—could come together for the glory of God and to advance the gospel.

We believe God wants us to dream big. It is a godly thing to have dreams and visions for a future that only God can accomplish. Imagine a church that is blessed with one thousand people coming to worship each weekend. The members of the church, along with the staff and elders, gather for a weekend of prayer. They plead with God to do a miracle in their church, and they ask the Lord to bring them twenty-five new people in the next ten years to join their church. Huh? They dream of growing by twenty-five people in ten years? That is definitely *not* a God-sized vision. God is not a small-dream God, and He does not call us to be small-dream people.

Get married. Have some kids. Buy a house. Be nice people. Take some trips. Enjoy grandkids. Our vision is too small!

Do you have dreams for your marriage and family that only God could accomplish? Have you ever considered, or dared to pray, that God would use you, as husband and wife, to impact the *world* for Christ? Geoffrey Botkin encouraged us to consider a 200-year dream, a dream which can only come to pass if God works a miracle of grace.[28] Your God-sized dream may be different. Here is ours.

We pray that God will use us to begin a Christian training ministry where people receive sixteen to twenty years of intense, personal discipleship. After this time of thorough training in the Scriptures and Christian living, each person would be mentored for the next thirty to fifty years. Here is where the dream gets truly "God-sized." Our dream is that in 200 years, God would use this discipleship plan to shape and develop 336,000 men and women for His purposes.[29] If 1% of these followers of Christ were pastors, that would mean 3,360 men serving in local churches.[30] If .5% were missionaries, there would be 1,680 people launched out to the remote parts of the earth. We also dream of these Christians giving generously of their money to their local churches and the global cause of Christ. If each of these people earned an average of $40,000 per year, and worked an average of 40 years, in 200 years over $53 billion would be given to strengthen local churches, agencies of compassion, and mission teams.

We told you this was a big dream! It is God-sized. Human effort and planning cannot accomplish it. It will take a miracle, and that is exactly what we are praying for. But let's be reasonable for a moment. Is a ministry dream like this even possible? We are only two people brought together in marriage.

Jesus looked at them and said, "With man this is impossible, but with God all things are possible."

MATTHEW 19:26

Here is our prayer for God to work this miracle:

God, would You work a miracle and lead our six children to know and love You with all their hearts? Would You then give each of our children, on average, six faithful children? Would You then give each of our grandchildren, on average, six faithful children? Would You continue this blessing, generation after generation, for the next 200 years? Let our descendents be spiritual arrows in Your hands, to advance Your Kingdom to the ends of the earth, until the Day of Your return. Amen!

A True Miracle

Will all of our children and grandchildren get married and have children? We don't know. God may call some of them to serve Him through singleness. Others may not be able to have children biologically, but may adopt or provide foster care for a dozen. We have no power or desire to manage the details, but we know that God created marriage with multi-generational Kingdom vision!

Can you now see why one of God's purposes for marriage is the raising of godly children? Consider how the impact changes when the numbers change. If the generational impact number is six, as we see above, in over 200 years God will have blessed the world with 336,000 of our descendents, who by God's grace will all love Him and serve Him. What if it were four? What if we had four children, and each of them, on average, had four children, and this repeated for the next 200 years? With that vision, instead of 336,000 people sharing God's love with the world, there would be 22,000. Perhaps 220 of them will be pastors, 110 missionaries, and $3.5 billion would be given.

What if there were but three faithful children per family, generation after generation? In 200 years, there would be 3,300 disciples. What if the average number of faithful children was merely two? In 200 years, there would only be 250. If there were only one child per generation, then in 200 years there would be seven people impacting the world for Christ.

Remember, the point here is *not* that people are unspiritual or not committed to God if they can't have children or have a small family. Instead, we want you to capture a God-sized vision for why He has chosen to bring you together in marriage. It isn't about you. It isn't just about your spouse. It isn't just about your kids. It is about *everyone* in your family understanding and embracing the fact that God has invited you into a global, multi-generational mission. You, your spouse, and your kids...your family is the tip of the spear!

Now hold on, here. What if the generational impact number were eight? What impact could your family have on the world if God blessed you with eight faithful children, and He worked a miracle and blessed each of them with eight faithful children, every generation for 200 years?

Over 200 years, 2,396,744 Christians would be launched in the world, living in the grace and truth of Jesus Christ. If 1% were pastors, that would be 23,967 pastors. If .5% were missionaries, 11,983 of your descendents would be bringing the gospel to people who may hear it for the first time. Do you care about poverty and helping meet needs around the world? Through your marriage and your *family ministry*, over $383 billion would have been given to the local church and to those in need. Let us put that in context. In 2006, the entire charitable giving in the United States, the nation that gives more than any other country in the world (both in total dollars and as a percentage of GDP) was $295 billion! [31]

> **Over 200 years, 2,396,744 Christians would be launched in the world, living in the grace and truth of Jesus Christ.**

The Visionary Marriage

Consider how God wants to grow and expand your vision for marriage. Where would you place yourself in this progression?

- **SELF FOCUSED:** Marriage is about me—I live for myself.

- **SPOUSE FOCUSED:** Marriage is about my spouse—I focus on his/her needs and growth.

- **MARRIAGE FOCUSED:** Marriage is about us—We seek to please God in and through our relationship.

- **CHILDREN FOCUSED:** Marriage is about our children—We share in our primary Christian ministry of passing faith and character to them.

- **KINGDOM FOCUSED:** Marriage is about our multi-generational mission—We focus on partnering with our children and grandchildren to participate in God's plan to fill the earth with worshippers.

Stepping Stones

When you have a visionary marriage, your vision extends beyond your marriage, and even beyond your children. We don't mean that your marriage and children are diminished, but rather you understand that being a Christian means giving your best to your marriage, and then as a couple giving your best to your children, knowing that you are participating in God's multi-generational mission. One of our favorite quotes has become a kind of mission statement for our family. It comes from William Bradford, who led the Pilgrims across the Atlantic on the Mayflower. In his journal, *Of Plymouth Plantation*, he explained the mission that drove them to move their church from Holland to the New World:

> **When you have a visionary marriage, your vision extends beyond your marriage, and even beyond your children.**

We cherish a great hope, and an inward zeal, of laying good foundations for the advance of the Gospel of the Kingdom of Christ to the remote parts of the earth, even if we should be but stepping stones to others in the performance of so great a work. [32]

By giving your best ministry to your spouse, and partnering together to impress the hearts of your children with a love for God, you are laying good foundations for the advance of the gospel of the kingdom of Jesus Christ to the remote parts of the earth. We pray that God would use our lives, our marriage, and our family as stepping stones to our descendents in the performance of so great a work!

Why are you married?

Here we are again, back at this question of purpose. Perhaps at the beginning of our journey you would have answered this question like most other couples. We love each other. We are compatible. We complete each other. Life is better together. Our prayer is that as you have walked through all of the Scripture passages in this book, God has given you a new and distinctively Christian answer. So what would you say? Why are you still married? We pray your answer will be something like this:

We are married because we are Christians, and we believe God has called us to be married, so we might help each other become more like Christ, and we might have the opportunity to impress the hearts of our children with a love for God. God has given us a shared mission of equipping the next generation to make a difference in this world for Christ, and they in turn would raise our grandchildren to know and love God. We remain committed to one another because we believe God wants to use our marriage to launch a massive multi-generational ministry that would shine for Christ in our neighborhood, our church, our nation, and to the ends of the earth.

Closing Prayer

Dear God,

It is amazing to me that despite our problems and in light of my sin, You still desire to use me, our marriage, and our family to advance Your Kingdom. I confess that my vision for our marriage and family has been too small. It is so easy for me to focus on just getting through each day, without keeping my heart and mind focused on why You brought our family together in the first place. Please make our family into a discipleship center. Please make it into an evangelism center. Give us multi-generational vision. Bless us with many grandchildren and great-grandchildren, and beyond, who love You with all their hearts. Begin with our marriage. Turn our hearts toward each other. Make the two of us one...to the ends of the earth all for the glory of God.

In Jesus' name, Amen.

Questions for further thought and discussion

1. Look back at the "five foci" for marriage. As we grow in Christ and in a biblical view of the world, our vision grows and expands. Up till now, where has your focus been?

2. In the last chapter, we talked about the biblical mission of raising godly children. How did seeing the multiplying generational numbers change your understanding of how parenting impacts the world?

3. How often do you think about your grandchildren and great-grandchildren? How would your marriage change if you spent more time praying together for them?

4. If you had to write a mission statement for your marriage and family, what would it be?

But from the beginning of creation, "God made them male and female." "Therefore a man shall leave his father and mother and hold fast to his wife, and the two shall become one flesh." So they are no longer two but one flesh. What therefore God has joined together, let not man separate.

Mark 10:6-9

Thank you for taking this journey of *Visionary Marriage*. Here are some ways you can keep growing together as a couple and as a family:

- Grow together with other couples as you learn through the *Visionary Marriage* DVD series.
- Get equipped to pass faith and character to your children by reading our companion book *Visionary Parenting* (Randall House, 2009), or use the *Visionary Parenting* DVD series. The video series is great for small groups and adult classes.
- Live Visionary Marriage and Visionary Parenting Conferences are also available. Hosting a live conference is a powerful way to impact your entire church with a Christian vision for family life.

To get more information about ordering DVD curriculum or hosting a live conference visit us online at www.VisionaryParenting.com or www.VisionaryMarriage.com.

ENDNOTES

[1] Luther's Works. Weimar Edition. Briefwechsel [Correspondence], vol. 3, pp. 81f.

[2] From D.L. Moody's sermon entitled, "The Christian's Warfare." - http://www.1timothy4-13.com/files/chr_vik/chrwarfare.html <http://www.1timothy4-13.com/files/chr_vik/chrwarfare.html>.

[3] D. James Kennedy, *What if Jesus Had Never Been Born* (Thomas Nelson Publishers: Nashville, TN, 1994) 14-16.

[4] Bob Lepine, *The Christian Husband* (Servant Publications: Ann Arbor, MI, 1999, p 169.

[5] Consider Financial Peace University at www.DaveRamsey.com.

[6] For an excellent and thorough book on this issue of "headship" as well as the biblical roles for men and women in the church, home, and society, we recommend *Recovering Biblical Manhood and Womanhood*, by Wayne Grudem and John Piper, published by Crossway Books, Wheaton, IL, 2008.

[7] Dr. Voddie Baucham was speaking on the subject of "Family Driven Faith."

[8] http://www.livescience.com/health/060524_longevity_research.html.

[9] http://www.psychpage.com/family/library/brwaitgalligher.html.

[10] Gilbert Bilezikian, *Beyond Sex Roles: What the Bible Says about a Woman's Place in Church and Family,* (Baker Academic, 3rd Edition, 2006).

[11] Noah Webster, *American Dictionary of the English Language (1828 Facsimile Edition)* (Foundation for American Christian Education: VA, 1967).

[12] If you are in an abusive situation, a marriage book is not the solution. Wives, husbands, and children can all be victims of abuse. If you or someone else in the family is in danger, quickly get help from your pastor, a local Christian counselor, or an abuse hotline.

[13] Dr. Emerson Eggerichs, *Love and Respect* (Integrity Publishers, 2004).

[14] Walter Bauer, *A Greek-English Lexicon of the New Testament and Other Early Christian Literature,* (University of Chicago Press: Chicago, 1979) 863.

[15] Robert Lewis, *Rocking the Roles,* (Nav Press: 1999).

[16] Bauer, 561.

[17] Voddie Baucham, *Family Driven Faith* (Crossway Books: Wheaton, IL. 2007) 161.

[18] In *Love and Respect*, Eggerichs calls this the "crazy cycle."

[19] Gary Thomas, *Sacred Marriage,* (Zondervan: Grand Rapids, MI, 2000).

[20]If a church chooses to develop a small group ministry, we recommend building groups around an age-integrated model where children and seniors of all ages are included. More information about age-integrated, family-integrated small groups is available in *Building a Home Centered Youth Ministry* available at www.VisionaryParenting.com.

[21]Rob Rienow, *Do Children Belong in Church: A Biblical Overview*, 2006. http://www.visionaryparenting.com/documents/do%20children%20belong%20in%20church.pdf.

[22]Equally important to worshipping together as a family at church, is worshipping together at home. God has given husbands and fathers the primary responsibility of leading family worship in the home, a command which is rooted in Deuteronomy 6 and Ephesians 6. We encourage you to read *Visionary Parenting* (Randall House, 2009) to get inspired and equipped how to take the lead in passing faith to your children through family worship.

[23]1 Peter 3:2 refers to a situation in which a believing wife is married to an unbelieving husband.

[24]For a foundational Bible study on this subject we recommend Rob's article "The Family and God's Plan for the World" located at http://www.visionaryparenting.com/vpchurch.htm.

[25]More information at www.demographicwinter.com.

[26]Rob Rienow, *Visionary Parenting* (Randall House Publishers: Nashville, TN, 2009). A DVD series of Visionary Parenting is also available for use in adult classes and small groups. More information at www.VisionaryParenting.com.

[27]Jacob Abbott, revised and edited by Michael J. McHugh, *Training Children in Godliness* (Christian Liberty Press: Arlington Heights, IL, 1992) 117.

[28]From sermon entitled *A 200 Year Plan: A Practicum on Multi-Generational Faithfulness*: San Antonio, TX. March 28, 2008.

[29]This number represents the total number of people from each of the seven generations. Not all these people would be alive at the same time.

[30]Numbers are rounded off.

[31]http://www.usatoday.com/news/nation/2007-06-25-charitable_N.htm.

[32]William Bradford, *Of Plymouth Plantation* (The Vision Forum, Inc: San Antonio, TX, 1999).

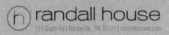